Table of Contents

1. About the Author

Sakshi Nagpal is a Salesforce architect deeply involved in the Salesforce community, with numerous Salesforce certifications to her name. With a fervent dedication to sharing knowledge and fostering innovation, she currently holds the position of Principal Architect at Ltimindtree. Sakshi has also earned recognition as an Einstein champion and has spoken at various Salesforce events and conferences. She resides in Canada with her wonderful husband and beloved child.

2. Compelling reasons to delve into this book.

- Attain a comprehensive grasp of data cloud consulting.
- Build a solid foundation in data cloud principles and practices.
- Explore the intersection of data and AI, crucial aspects of modern professional landscapes.
- Boost your marketability and career paths within the Salesforce ecosystem.
- Unlock opportunities for career advancement and entrepreneurial ventures in data management and analytics.
- The future belongs to those companies who use their data well. And Data Cloud is an amazing tool that can enable this.

3. Introduction

Geoffrey Moore once said: "Without big data you are blind and deaf and in the middle of freeway".

Data cloud has revolutionized the Salesforce ecosystem. The main purpose of Data Cloud is to understand and act upon customer data to drive more relevant experiences and harmonize data from multiple sources with a standardized and extendable data model.

 With this book, you can embark on a fascinating journey through the intertwined worlds of computer science, Salesforce, and the dynamic collaboration between Steve Fisher and the visionary Marc Benioff.

Imagine Silicon Valley in the late 1970s, where a young Fisher and Benioff teamed up to create software games for the cutting-edge Apple Inc. and Atari computers. This early foray into the tech landscape set the stage for their shared passion. As fate would have it, their paths diverged temporarily when Fisher pursued Computer Science subject at Stanford and Benioff pursued Business Studies subject at the University of Southern California.

The narrative took an exciting turn in 2004 when Fisher and Benioff's trajectories converged once again. Fisher's entry into Salesforce, after stints at Apple, AT&T, and a startup he co-founded, marked a significant chapter in his journey.

A decade later, having spearheaded technical design and development at Salesforce, Fisher assumed the role of Chief Technology Officer at eBay. However, the allure of innovation and the evolving tech landscape called him back to Salesforce in 2021.

Today, Fisher stands at the forefront, guiding the development of the next generation of CRM and unified data services. He notably leads the creation of Salesforce Data Cloud, a real-time hyperscale data engine that integrates information from diverse sources, crafting a comprehensive view of the customer.

Steve Fisher's story is more than a career; it's an odyssey through the ever-evolving landscape of technology, where passion, collaboration, and the pursuit of innovation converge to shape the future of data integration.

Steve Fisher Once aptly remarked: *"Data Cloud makes bringing whatever data you want into Salesforce data easy. By unifying and harmonizing that data, it creates a golden record that contains all the information about your customers, your orders, cases, vehicles, or whatever entity you choose".*

Salesforce's CDP offering has undergone several name changes: from Customer 360 Audiences to Salesforce CDP, then to Marketing Cloud Customer Data Platform and now it is referred to as Salesforce Data Cloud.

Comparison between Data Cloud and Salesforce platform

Data Cloud objects can ingest and store much larger volumes of data (in the magnitude of billions of records) compared to regular custom and standard objects on the Salesforce Platform.

Standard/Custom objects are designed for transactional use cases and are not suitable for storing and processing big data. On the other hand, Data Cloud objects add data lake house-like capabilities.

Another key distinction is that Data Cloud objects do not support Synchronous Apex triggers. However, you can still achieve process automation by subscribing to <u>Change Data Capture</u> (CDC) and utilizing Flows or Apex. What's common between the Data Cloud objects and the platform objects is that they are built on the same metadata-driven foundation, making it possible to use platform features, such as Salesforce Flow, Apex, and Platform Events.

Advantages of Data Cloud

Improved Data Management Capabilities: Salesforce Data Cloud enhances the data management capabilities of enterprises by enabling them to purify, integrate, and consolidate duplicate records. This leads to a reduction in manual efforts for businesses, streamlining data processes and workflows, and improving data accuracy and quality. Consequently, organizations can save time and resources, enabling their teams to concentrate on strategic initiatives and higher-value tasks.

As you can see in the above example-: Data cloud has reconciliation rules and matching Rules. These rules help in consolidating data. Data cloud gets data from multiple sources and consolidates it. Data Cloud can provide complete view of Customer. Data Cloud can also be source of truth for an Exterprise.

Comprehensive Customer Insights: A key feature of Data Cloud is its ability to offer unified, comprehensive customer information. On top of that with that Data Cloud provides **calculated insights and Streaming insights**. These insights empower companies to adopt a data-driven culture and make more informed business decisions and act on it.

Effortless Integration: Unlocking the versatility of Data Cloud involves effortless integration of data through connectors and federating with prominent big data providers. This process occurs securely and in compliance with regulations. External data platforms such as Snowflake, Google, AWS, and Databricks seamlessly participate in this ecosystem. Notably, the integration can also be achieved with **zero-copy or zero-ETL (Extract, Transform, Load) methodologies,** facilitating streamlined and efficient data sharing and AI model training. Data Cloud has numerous connectors that make Data Cloud an extensible and limitless platform.

Improved Personalization & Conversion Rates: By leveraging enriched and well-organized customer profiles containing behavioral and other data, the Salesforce Data Cloud assists businesses in enhancing their targeted marketing campaigns. This is achieved through delivering personalized messages and recommendations, ultimately leading to increased customer engagement and conversion rates, thereby elevating return on investment (ROI).

Scalability & Agility: Utilizing the Salesforce platform, businesses can easily adapt to and meet evolving market needs by offering scalability and agility. This enables them to **handle large volumes of data** in line with the increasing volume of customer interactions. Consequently, companies can scale their business operations without compromising efficiency and achieve optimal ROI.

Decoupling Data from Application Stacks: Enterprises are currently facing the challenge of liberating their data from the application-centric silos that have evolved over the years. The emergence of a new wave of data aggregation vendors like Snowflake, Databricks, Confluent, and others attests to this growing trend. For Salesforce, the task is to expose and consolidate data not only from its applications but also from various other sources. This ensures alignment with the broader industry trend.

Security: With Data Cloud data remains within Salesforce environment, ensuring it is in safe hands.

- **Simplified Data Management**: Data Lakes free you from the complexity and constraints of defining a schema and mapping it accordingly. It stores your data "as is" which can include images, videos, documents, audio, etc.
- **Better Traceability**: Data Lake makes it easy to trace data since the stored data is managed better throughout its entire lifecycle from data definition, access, and storage to processing, and analytics. Moreover, in a Data Lake, you can add as many users as you like without compromising on the performance.
- **Democratized Access**: When you use Data Cloud, you get rid of independent data silos and bureaucratic boundaries between business processes. Every user is empowered to access select or all enterprise data if they have the required permissions.

4. Data Cloud Administration

At Dreamforce 2023 it was announced that Enterprise Edition and above customers could access the Free Data Cloud. Starting September 19th, 2023, Enterprise Edition and above customers can initiate Data Cloud Provisioning at no cost by signing up under Your Account. However, segmentation and activation is not available with free data cloud subscription. To see exactly what it offers check this-: https://help.salesforce.com/s/articleView?id=000396380&type=1

Data Cloud can be provisioned on a home organization or on a standalone Data Cloud organization.

To enable Data Cloud on a Salesforce Org, user should go to Data Cloud Setup -> Home and then click on Get started.

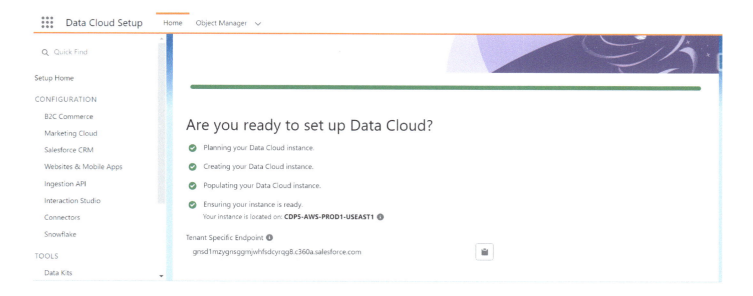

For Managing Data Cloud there are two permission sets -:

1. Data Cloud Admin
2. Data Cloud Marketing Admin

If the customer wants to create a target audience based on customer lifetime value, the following steps can be followed in the data cloud: If the customer wants to create a target audience based on customer lifetime value, following steps can be followed in Data Cloud:

• Ingest Data from Source->Map ingested data to Data Model object in data cloud -> Create Calculation insight-> Use in segmentation

Moreover Einstein, Flow, Lightning, and Apex can connect with data Cloud natively and easily supercharge their business applications with powerful AI. What this means is that Tableau also natively connects to Data Cloud, instantly analyzing data with the click of a button and acting with AI-powered insights in the flow of work.

When Data Cloud App is opened from App launcher below tabs are available-:

Data streams- This Tab shows different Source systems from where data comes to Data Cloud. New Source systems can be added via this tab.

Data Lake Objects- This tab contains Structure and fields of data Lake Objects. Mapping can also be done from this tab. Data Lake objects can be mapped to Data Model Objects from this tab. These Objects are designed to store bulk data.

Data Model Objects- New Data Model Objects can be created from this tab.

Data Explorer- Used to see actual data in Data Lake Objects, Calculated Insights and Data Model Objects and Graphs. The data is grouped by Data space.

Data Explorer retrieves up to 100 records of DMOs or DLOs per query. Therefore, if we want to check more records use Query API or Direct API can be used.

Columns displayed can be adjusted, and there is also an option to copy the SQL.

Identity Resolution tab-: Match rules and identity resolution rules can be created to unify data from different source systems.

Segments-Segments(Categories) can be created based on unified data and Profiles.

Activation target-This tab shows target systems. Golden records can

be published to these target systems to be actioned upon.

Example-: Marketing Cloud (Data Extension).

Activations-Segments can be activated via this tab. Targets are also specified for each activation

Example Segment,

Calculation Insights- Generate insights like Lifetime value of Customer on unified data.

Data Action-

Data Transforms-: Transforms can be used to clean the ingested data that comes from the Source systems. This allows to transform Data Lake Object and Data model Objects by using Batch transform or Streaming Data transform.

New Data Transform

Choose a type of data transform

Batch Data Transform

Use a visual editor to modify your data as needed or at scheduled intervals.

Streaming Data Transform

Use SQL to process your data in near-real time

Data Spaces- Data spaces are a group of Data. Data Spaces provide an efficient means of managing different datasets within a single instance of Data Cloud. The concept is like business unit in marketing cloud. As of now 50 Dara Spaces can be created in a Data Cloud Account.

Profile   Explorer-:This   tab   is   used   to   Manage   Profiles   in   Data   Cloud.

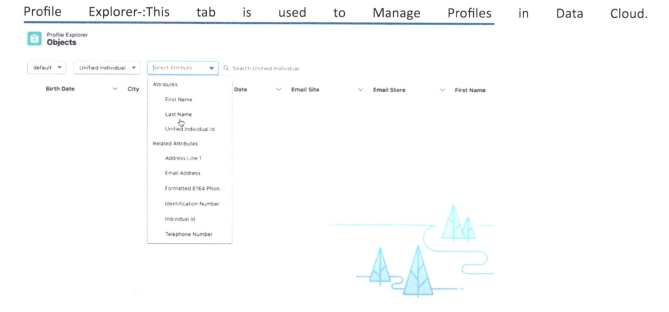

Control Event Notification in Data Cloud

Control event notifications can be used to monitor the processes and data flow in the Data Cloud platform.

A record triggered flow can be created for below mentioned objectss. And user can be notified if Segmentation failed to run or Activation was not published.

- Data Stream
- Segment
- Activation
- Identity Resolution

- Calculated Insights

Sharing rules can be created in data cloud for Streams, segments, calculation insights etc.

5. Data Cloud and AI

The benefit of consolidating all data into a singular data cloud platform lies in the ability to introduce a unified governance layer that facilitates interactions between AI and data. Within the new platform architecture, this governing element is referred to as the Einstein Trust Layer.

Below are Einstein Trust layer principles-:

Doc link-: https://www.salesforce.com/eu/blog/meet-salesforces-trusted-ai-principles/

Consider having access to an intelligent personal assistant known for its accuracy and factual responses. However, there's a catch: for every five correct responses, there's one that appears accurate but contains false information. Can you trust such an assistant with critical tasks?

A prime illustration of this scenario occurs when a user employs such a model to plan a holiday. The user requests the model to recommend hotels with specific requirements. Subsequently, the model generates a search query and utilizes it to conduct a web search, retrieving a list of web pages containing information about matching hotels. The text from these web pages is parsed and sent back to the model through in-context learning with the information included in the next prompt. The Language Model (LM) then employs its pre-trained weights to identify relevant information based on the user's initial input. It can then summarize the results and allow the user to chat with it about them.

Therefore, the actual web search results of hotels are used for grounding — using the search hotel context to give factual responses based upon real hotels returned in the search. In addition any inserted citations and references from the web search results, can give the user additional confidence as they can click through to view the external data used for grounding and compare this to the output of the model before booking the hotel.

A vendor's state-of-the-art offerings often outpace the current status of many of its customers. Within the Salesforce user base, there are still those who have not adopted the Lightning interface introduced a decade ago. Challenges persist for customers managing multiple instances, struggling to establish seamless connections across them. Additionally, a substantial number have yet to migrate to the AWSbased Hyperforce infrastructure. It's not a lack of willingness but rather a lack of a compelling reason to bear the costs and efforts associated with upgrades.

In an era where CEOs urge IT leaders to craft AI roadmaps, AI becomes a catalyst for IT modernization. The introduction of Data Cloud, facilitating data consolidation, contributes to building a business case for modernization.

Keith Block while commenting on Data Cloud expresses his enthusiasm, stating, "I couldn't be more in love with this product. This is truly an incredible unlock." The platform addresses the complexity faced by companies managing numerous systems in the past. With Data Cloud, integration becomes a straightforward process, allowing data to seamlessly flow and coordinate based on the canonical data model. This enables companies to effortlessly obtain critical account data, a valuable application for any business.

Another noteworthy aspect is that customer data remains within the Salesforce ecosystem. At a time when data is separating from applications, there is a risk for Salesforce, as well as other vendors, that customers might opt to keep their data in a separate store, making it easier to switch to alternative applications. However, it could also present an opportunity for Salesforce to expand its reach beyond traditional CRM territory and become the preferred platform for back-office and operational data. Schmaier emphasizes that Salesforce is focusing on partnerships with data companies rather than aiming to replace them. He acknowledges the multi-lake world, indicating that while operational data may integrate into Data Cloud, he doesn't foresee customers moving their CRM data to a different platform.

Schmaier envisions a future in which individuals may initially lean towards more complex data warehousing technologies but eventually favor the convenience of an out-of-the-box solution. The objective is to offer a comprehensive solution that encompasses operational data from both the front and mid-office, aligning with the broader ambitions beyond CRM. The integration of data and AI remains a critical piece in this evolving landscape.

Data Cloud provides the data and foundation for Einstein Copilot, our new generative AI conversational assistant, along with Einstein Copilot Builder, an innovative platform for building and customizing AI assistants, enabling the development of a new era of AI-powered applications. Utilizing Data Cloud, we can generate a data graph that offers a consolidated, real-time view of a customer or any entity. Additionally, with a single click, customers can effortlessly transmit all pertinent data to the prompt, which subsequently feeds into the LLM. There's no need to send SQL queries or manually create data joins.

The AI features mentioned above are Pilot features, and purchase decision in Salesforce should be based solely on existing features rather than the future roadmap of Salesforce. Therefore, purchase decisions should not rely on upcoming features.

With Einstein Studio, large language models (LLM) can be utilized, allowing users to create custom AI models from a variety of predictive or generative AI services. This concept is known as BYOM (Bring Your Own Model). Other AI model providers include Vertex AI (Google), Amazon SageMaker, OpenAI (also known as Chat GPT), Claude (Anthropic), and numerous others.

Salesforce's LLM leverages Data Cloud or can be plugged into a different data lake. You can see this is a flexible, mix n' match way of working with GenAI with your Salesforce data.

Below diagram from Salesforce documentation shows how external AI models can be used with Salesforce:link-:https://developer.salesforce.com/blogs/2023/08/bring-your-own-ai-models-tosalesforce-with-einstein-studio

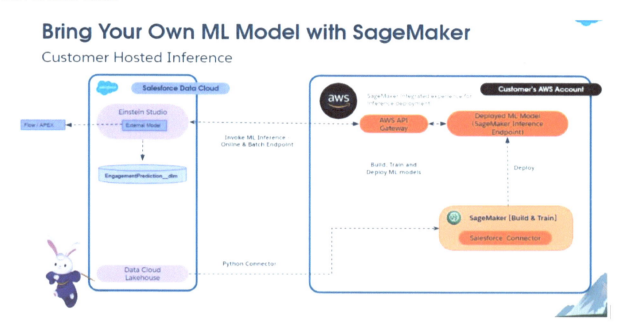

In the Case studies section I have included a case study for using creating an AI model is AWS and consuming it in salesforce. In the case studies section . This is the third case study.

6. Data Cloud Architecture

Operating within the Salesforce platform and being confined to Oracle as the underlying storage mechanism can present limitations. Challenges may arise, especially when dealing with unstructured data, managing trillions of records, or handling objects with an extensive array of fields. Addressing these issues involves a comprehensive reconstruction of the core metadata layer. The goal is to abstract the underlying storage mechanism, transitioning from a structure that complements the transactional database, Oracle, to adopting a more versatile data lakehouse architecture. In this architecture, the data lake plays a pivotal role, establishing a connection to enhance overall flexibility and functionality.

Susainah Plaisted has written a very informative blog on data Cloud Architecture, the facts presented about data cloud architecture are based on the insights provided in the blog.

Data Cloud includes multiple services, encompassing DynamoDB for hot storage so data is supplied fast, Amazon S3 for cold storage, and a SQL metadata store for indexing all metadata

Below is a brief description of these components:

Dynamo DB has following features:

- Fully managed, highly available with replicas
- Scales to massive workloads, distributed server less database
- Millions of requests per second,100 TB's of storage
- Fast and consistent in storage
- Data partitioning allows faster reads/writes.
- And large volume of data can be Ingested.

Amazon S3

Amazon S3 is a fundamental building block of AWS, offering infinitely scalable storage solutions. It is utilized across various use cases including backup and storage, disaster recovery, archiving, application hosting, media hosting, and big data analytics.

SQL Database

SQL database and indexes help in fast retrieval of metadata

Data Cloud securely stores all its data in a data lakehouse, utilizing a Parquet file format stored within S3 buckets. The underlying technology relies on Apache Parquet, which employs a columnar file storage format. Unlike the row-oriented CSV data format, Parquet is specially designed to efficiently handle large sets of complex data.

Below are some features of Parquet File Format:

- Data compression: Parquet files utilize encoding and compression algorithms to minimize memory usage, enhancing efficiency.

- Columnar storage: In analytical workloads, rapid data retrieval is crucial, making columnar storage vital. However, we'll explore this further later in the article.

- Language agnostic: As previously mentioned, developers can employ various programming languages to interact with data in Parquet files.

- Open-source format: Parquet is an open-source format; ensuring users aren't restricted to a particular vendor.

- Support for complex data types: Parquet provides support for a wide range of complex data types, facilitating versatile data handling.

In traditional, row-based storage, the data is stored as a sequence of rows, as illustrated below:

	Product	Customer	Country	Date	Purchase Amount
Row1	Hockey	John Smith	USA	1/1/2024	100
Row2	Sofa	John Smith	USA	1/2/2024	200
Row3	Shoes	Michael Jackson	Canada	1/4/2024	300
Row4	Shirt	Joana_Singh	India	1/5/2024	400
Row5	Cupboard	Mariam	UK	1/3/2024	500

Now, when we are talking about OLAP scenarios, some of the common questions that your users may ask are:

- How many items/products did we sell?
- How many users from the USA bought Shirt?
- What is the total amount spent by customer John Smith?

- How many sales did we have on 3rd January 2024?

Answering this question is difficult for row-based storage. Let's now examine how the column store works. As you may assume, the approach is 180 degrees different:

Column 1	Column 2	Column3	Column4	Column5
Product	Customer	Country	Date	Purchase Amount
Hockey	John Smith	USA	1/1/2024	100
Sofa	John Smith	USA	1/2/2024	200
Shoes	Michael Jackson	Canada	1/4/2024	300
Shirt	Joana Singh	India	1/5/2024	400
Cupboard	Mariam	UK	1/3/2024	500

Each column is physically separated from other columns! Going back to our previous business question: the engine can now scan only those columns that are needed by the query (product and country) while skipping scanning the unnecessary columns. And, in most cases, this should improve the performance of the analytical queries.

Data cloud supports following objects:
- Data Source Object (DSO) — the original data source in the original file format.
- Data Lake Object (DLO) — the data after it has been transformed and stored in the data lake in the Parquet format.
- Data Model Object (DMO) — the data after it has been mapped to the Salesforce metadata structure.

Let me state in simple words:
1. Data Source Object (DSO): This is where the data journey begins – the original data in its original format. Consider it as the raw information right from the source. Data source object has the same fields as the source.

These sources can either be:
- Salesforce platforms including Sales Cloud, Commerce Cloud, Marketing Cloud and Marketing Cloud Personalization
- Object storage platforms including Amazon S3, Microsoft Azure Storage and Google Cloud Storage

- Ingestion APIs and Connector SDKs to programmatically load data from websites, mobile apps and other systems. This connector supports only insert statements and a single request cannot exceed 200 KB of data
- SFTP for file based transfer

2. Data Lake Object (DLO): After a bit of magic or transformation the data moves to the DLO. Here, it is stored in a format called Parquet, making it organized and ready for use.

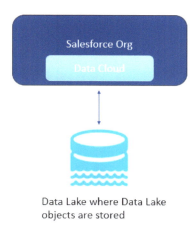

Data Lake where Data Lake
objects are stored

3. Data Model Object (DMO): Now, the data gets mapped to fit into Salesforce's structure. It is like giving the data a new outfit that suits the style of Salesforce's metadata structure. This makes it seamlessly work within Salesforce.

Data Cloud accommodates both structured and unstructured data. However, its true strength lies in its ability to structure this data through a transformative process. To facilitate this transformation, three new types of objects have been introduced, and it is crucial to familiarize yourself with them.

Data Cloud objects don't directly interact with Synchronous Apex triggers; you can still automate processes by subscribing to Change Data Capture (CDC) and utilizing Flows or Apex. What's intriguing is that Data Cloud objects and platform objects share a common foundation—they both rely on the same metadata-driven structure. This means you can utilize platform features like Salesforce Flow, Apex, and Platform Events for both types of objects. It's akin to having a shared toolkit that seamlessly operates across different aspects of your Salesforce data.

Data Cloud leverages industry-standard formats such as the following:

- Parquet: An open-source format supported by other cloud providers like Snowflake. Unlike traditional data lakes data, Data Cloud supports both batch and streaming events.
- Iceberg: Another community-driven open-source format.
- Live query functionality enables other data lakes, such as Snowflake, to query the data in Data Model Objects (DMOs) without the need to move or copy the data.

These guidelines facilitate the integration of external platforms with Data Cloud through zero-copy architecture, such as Snowflake, enabling seamless connectivity. Data on Data Cloud, allowing users to take actions based on insights gained from it.

Role of Apache Iceberg serves as an abstraction layer positioned between the physical data files and their organization to construct a table. This technology is compatible with various data processing frameworks such as Apache Spark and Apache Presto, as well as high-performance query services like Amazon Athena and Amazon EMR. The integration of these technologies collectively facilitates the effective management of record-level updates and enables the execution of SQL queries within the Data Cloud data lakehouse.

7. Ingesting Data in Data Cloud

Data ingestion involves retrieving data from the source system in its raw format and temporarily storing it in Source Objects. A Data Stream is directed into a Data Source Object, or 'DSO,' serving as a temporary storage space for the data in its raw form, akin to a CSV file. Simple transformations can be applied to fields during the data entry process. We can obtain all the required fields from source system. This allows for the option to return to the initial data structure if any errors occur or if there are adjustments to business requirements during the setup process. Additionally, it is possible to expand the dataset by introducing extra formula fields for tasks such as refining nomenclature or executing row based calculations. Each source system will be depicted as a data stream in Data Cloud.

Below are some examples source systems that can be selected for building a new Stream.

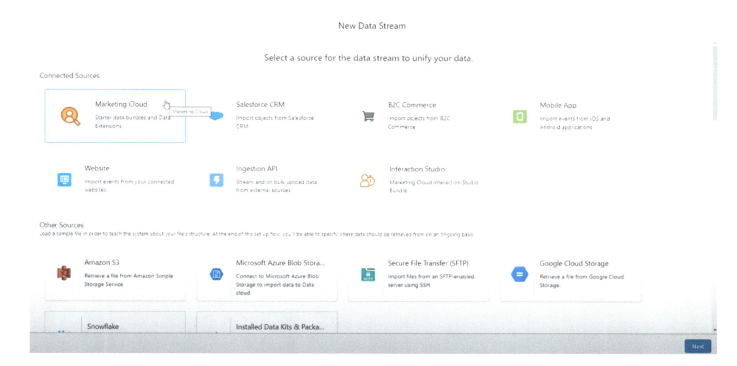

Unless your data is sourced from a raw data lake, it makes sense to keep the raw data history. Data lake object is automatically created from a Data Source object.

For example, if a customer's loyalty hotel points and loyalty airline points are stored together in the same record in Sales Clouds, it is a better option to store these points in separate records for better tracking. Therefore, before ingesting data, the object model should be optimized in the source system.

Customer has one to one relation with loyalty points table.

Customer Id	Hotel points	Airline points
1234	50	75

Below is a better option. Customer has one to much relationship with Loyalty points table.

Customer Id	Hotel points	Airline points
1234	50	
1234		75

Formatting phone number to make the format consistent is another use case where data should be corrected in source systems before ingesting data.

The following mistakes should be avoided when planning data ingestion for Data Cloud:

Lack of Metadata Management: Metadata elucidates crucial relationships within data, aiding users, data experts, and automation tools in locating, utilizing, managing, and reusing data to maximize its value. Without effective metadata management in your data lakes, data lacks context, rendering data governance and quality attainment challenging, thus rendering it unsuitable for use.

Poor Data Governance: Data governance ensures the tracking, maintenance, and quality of data ingested into data lakes. Absence of defined data governance policies and quality standards complicates data governance efforts, resulting in the accumulation of useless and irrelevant data within your data lake.

Data Swamps vs. Data Lakes: Data lakes contain well-organized, flexible, and relevant data, whereas data swamps consist of outdated and irrelevant data lacking organization. Transparent evaluation of data prior to ingestion establishes its relevance to business needs, thus preventing the accumulation of unnecessary data. Without regular audits to assess data relevance and accuracy in your data lake, it can quickly become inundated with irrelevant, unclean data, diminishing its value for business decisions.

Lack of Automation: Data lakes accommodate vast amounts of data in various raw formats, continuously ingesting data from diverse sources. Lack of automation tools for monitoring and managing data in your data lakes hampers organization, data management, and governance, potentially leading to the creation of a data swamp.

Ingestion has 3 main steps-:Ingest, Initiate and transform

Transformation of Data after Ingestion-:

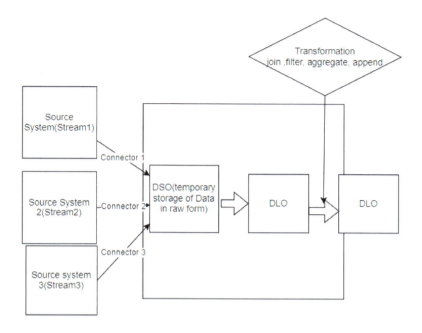

Data can be sourced from multiple source systems.Incoming data is temporarily stored in DSO. And then ,data is housed in Data Lake objects which can store millions of records.If transfomation is required,then joins,filters can be applied to Data Lake object and result can be stored in another Data Lake object.The transformed data Lake object can be mapped to Data Model objects.

Source Systems

We can ingest data to Salesforce Data Cloud from following source systems:

- Traditional software

- External databases

- CRM

- Ecommerce

- Data lakes

- Marketing and email databases

- Customer service

- Digital engagement data (including web and mobile)

- Analytics

When you obtain data from a source system, consider the following:

- Identify primary key and foreign keys.

- Identify any foreign keys present in the data set. These additional keys in the source may link to the primary key of a different data set. For example, the sales order details data set contains a product ID that corresponds to the item purchased. This product ID links to a whole separate table with more details about that product, such as color or size. The instance of product ID on the sales order details data set is the foreign key, and the instance of product ID on the product data set is the primary key.

- Ascertain whether the data is immutable, meaning it does not change once a record is transmitted, or if the dataset requires the capability to accommodate updates to existing records. While setting up data stream, the mode is set to full refresh(data will be overridden with new data from source) or upsert(data will be upserted from source)

- Apply transformation to source data

- For instance, you can utilize basic formulas to cleanse names or execute row-based calculations.

- Review the attributes, or fields that come from each data source; identify the source of truth for the data and get data from most recently updated and accurate source.

- Ensure that authentication details are readily accessible to access each dataset.

Data Cloud Connectors-:

Data is retrieved from source using connectors. Below are some OOTB connectors that are available in data Cloud: These connectors can be configured via configuration,without writing code.

- Cloud Storage Connector

- Google Cloud Storage Connector

- B2C Commerce Connector

- Marketing Cloud Personalization Connector

- Marketing Cloud Engagement Data Sources and Connector

- Salesforce CRM Connector

- Web and Mobile Application Connector

The Refresh History tab serves as a valuable resource for validating that data is being retrieved as the expected cadence and without errors. Connectors can be configured from data Cloud setup.

Below table gives OOTB connectors and their features-:

Connector	Source System	Frequency and refresh mode	Considerations

Amazon S3 Storage Connector	Amazon Web Services S3	• Hourly, daily weekly monthly (batches of data)	Single Data Cloud org can connect to multiple S3 buckets
Google Cloud Storage Connector	Google Cloud Storage (GCS), is an online file based storage web service. Flat files can be ingested.	• Periodic transfer of batches of data. • Hourly sync • Upsert or Full refresh	You need your GCS file and source details to ingest data. Periodically conducts an automated data transfer of active objects 5 GCS connections per org are supported
B2C Commerce Connector	B2C commerce instance	• Sales Order and Sales Order Customer-Hourly. • Others-Daily • Data Stream that brings in Sales order data from b2c Commerce can be refreshed using Upsert mode. • For Other data Full refresh is available	• Activation Targets are automatically created. • The B2C Commerce • Connector ingests 30 days of historical data. • B2C commerce instance •
Marketing Cloud Personalization Connector	Marketing cloud business unit	• Data Stream that contains profile data can be refreshed every 15 mins. • Data stream that contains Event/Engagement data can be refreshed every 2 mins.	• The Marketing Cloud Connector is a functionality enabling the streaming of data from Marketing Cloud to Data Cloud in near Realtime. This

			connector utilizes. Automation Studio to schedule and execute data extracts from Marketing Cloud data extensions, forwarding them to Data Cloud via SFTP (Secure File Transfer Protocol). •
Marketing Cloud Engagement Data Sources and Connector	Connect to a Marketing cloud business unit	You can configure the frequency and time of the data extracts in Automation Studio	• Activation target is automatically created for this connector. • Consists of email and mobile engagement data (including Einstein engagement data) • Data from any data extension can be ingested through this

			connector. Engagement data like clicks, open can also be ingested.
Salesforce CRM Connector		• Data streams whose frequency is **Hourly** their refresh mode can be Full or Upsert. • Data Stream whose frequency is **Weekly** their mode must be Full refresh.	• You can select one object per data stream. • Multiple Salesforce orgs can be connected to data Cloud org. • Salesforce org can be connected to multiple Data Cloud orgs.
Web and mobile Connector	Capture real time events from brands website.	• Data Stream that contains profile data can be refreshed every 15 mins. • Data stream that contains Event/Engagement data can be refreshed every 2 mins.	• This connector collects online data from websites and mobile apps. • Using this connector, trigger actions can be created based on real time behavior on any channel-Email,SMS, Push notification.
Ingestion API Or MuleSoft(using Ingestion API)	Ingestion API can has two patterns- 1. Streaming 2. Bulk	15 minutes(near real time)	

New Connectors can be configured from Data Cloud Setup

New CRM Connectors can be configured using following screen-:

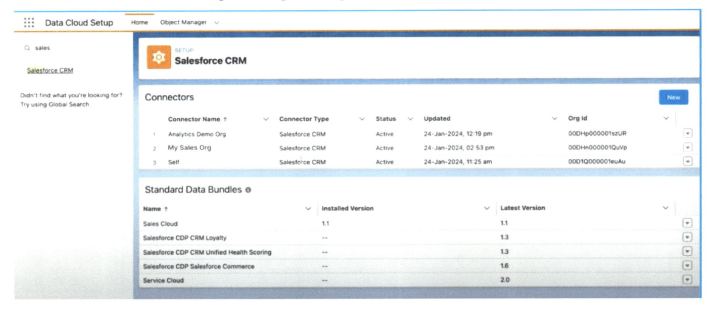

If we click on New Salesforce CRM Connectors, we get following options-:

Connect an Org

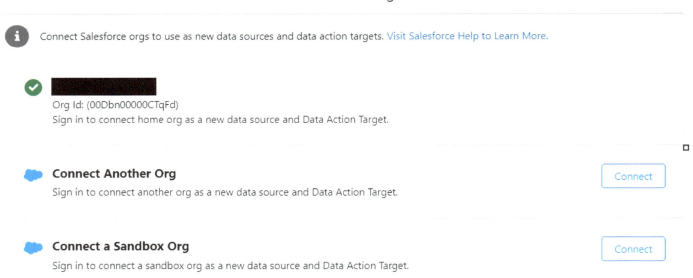

Connect Salesforce orgs to use as new data sources and data action targets. Visit Salesforce Help to Learn More.

Org Id: (00Dbn00000CTqFd)
Sign in to connect home org as a new data source and Data Action Target.

Connect Another Org
Sign in to connect another org as a new data source and Data Action Target.

Connect

Connect a Sandbox Org
Sign in to connect a sandbox org as a new data source and Data Action Target.

Connect

When setting the connector for Amazon S3 connector following connection details are required-:

New Amazon S3 Source

* Connection Name   * Connection API Name

[Enter connection name...]   [Enter connection API name...]

Authentication Details

* AWS access key   * AWS secret access key

[Enter AWS access key.]   [Enter AWS secret access key.]

Connection Details

* Bucket Name   * Parent Directory ⓘ

[Enter Bucket Name]   [/]

[Test Connection]

[Back]   [Save]

Sharing rules can be created in data cloud for Streams, segments, calculation insights etc.

Ingestion API and Ingestion API connector-:

If you want to personalize your connection to other data sources, you have the option to utilize the Ingestion API. With this API, you can craft a connector, upload your schema, and establish data streams within your organization. These streams can be set to update incrementally or in bulk, depending on the configuration of your API requests. Ingestion API can also be used for legacy systems and on-premise systems.

Ingestion API connector is available in Data Cloud setup.

Ingestion API can be used to insert bulk data or to get data in near real time.

Bulk API

- Moving large amounts of Data on a daily, weekly or monthly schedule
- It can be used to load historic Data.

Streaming API

Source system built on modern streaming architectures.

- Change data capture events.
- Consuming data from webhooks.
- Small micro batches of records being updated in near real time.

Steps to Configure Ingestion API-:

1) Go to Data Cloud Setup->Ingestion API and click on New. Give a name to the API.
2) Upload schema by clicking on Upload Files button.
   - Schema file should adhere to Open API specification.

     For more information, see https://www.openapis.org.

     For more information on how to create this file and what it should contain, check this-:

     https://help.salesforce.com/s/articleView?id=sf.c360_a_ingestion_api_schema_req.htm&type=5

Example of schema file with 3 objects-: Order,OrderItem,SalesCustomer.

```
openapi: 3.0.3
components:
 schemas:
  Order:
   type: object
   properties:
    contact_name:
     type: string
    created_date:
     type: string
     format: date-time
```

```
        type: string
  OrderItem:
    type: object
    properties:
      cost:
        type: number
      name:
        type: string
      orderId:
        type: string
      itemNumber:
        type: number
  SalesCustomer:
    type: object
    properties:
      address:
        type: string
      age:
        type: number
      city:
        type: string
      country:
        type: string
```

Once schema is uploaded. The schema contents like Objects/Entities and their corresponding fields are listed in the schema-:

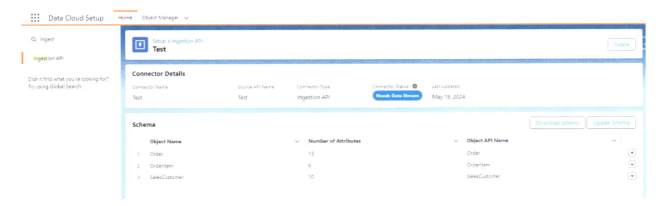

3) Open Data Stream tab from App Launcher, and create a new Stream.Create a Data stream of type Ingestion API.

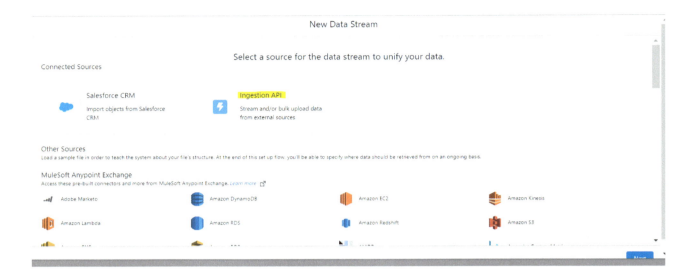

Then select the name of Ingestion API and select the objects that should be mapped-:

For each object select the Category, Primary key and Event Time field-:

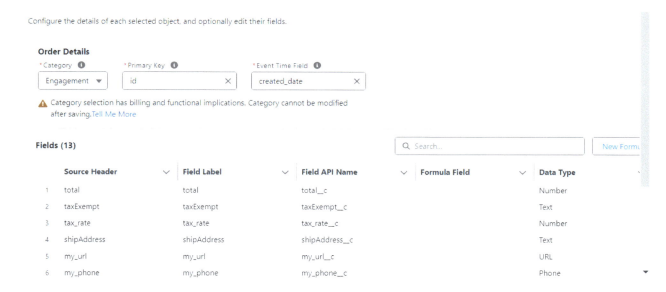

Configure the details of each selected object, and optionally edit their fields.

Order Details

*Category ⓘ	*Primary Key ⓘ	*Event Time Field ⓘ
Engagement ▼	id ✕	created_date ✕

⚠ Category selection has billing and functional implications. Category cannot be modified after saving.Tell Me More

Fields (13)   🔍 Search...   New Form

	Source Header ⌄	Field Label ⌄	Field API Name ⌄	Formula Field ⌄	Data Type
1	total	total	total__c		Number
2	taxExempt	taxExempt	taxExempt__c		Text
3	tax_rate	tax_rate	tax_rate__c		Number
4	shipAddress	shipAddress	shipAddress__c		Text
5	my_url	my_url	my_url__c		URL
6	my_phone	my_phone	my_phone__c		Phone

Also, app exchange also contains diverse Data cloud connectors.

Authentication for Ingestion API-:

1) First step is to acquire access token-:

2) Second step it to get Data Cloud token by exchanging the access token(Access token from first step).

3) Third step is to use Data Cloud access token to communicate with Data Cloud(tenant specific URL)

Zero-ETL Approach-:

If data needs to be accessed without storing data into Salesforce Data Cloud, then zero-ETL approach should be considered. According to Salesforce Newsletter- This zero-ETL approach guarantees real-time access to the latest data from snowflake data while maintaining the highest standards of security and governance. This eliminates the necessity for maintaining traditional ETL tools, streamlining the data management and reducing operational costs. For example, a data scientist can build AI models in Snowflake to determine customer product interests in the last quarter. By joining Salesforce objects such as profiles, website visits, and POS Data with Snowflake's product interest data, they can unlock new insights.

Fully Qualified key

When integrating a source system, mapped fields must include primary keys and foreign keys. For instance, in a Salesforce CRM Cloud instance, the source of truth for Contact data resides in the MDM system. Marketing Cloud also serves as a source system, where the Subscriber key corresponds to the MDM Id.

When you map data from Salesforce CRM, then the following fields must be mapped. This will help when unifying profiles between two source systems.

Primary key- Record Id

Foreign key- MDM Id

FirstName	LastName	Email	Phone	MDM Id(External id)	Record Id
John	Smith	John.smith@gmail.com	437-4278989	20231204000012	003Hs00004YCaMglAL

Data Stream

A data stream is an entity that can be extracted from a data source — for example, 'Orders' from Commerce Cloud, 'Contacts' from Sales Cloud, or 'subscribers' from Marketing Cloud. Once a data source is connected to Data Cloud, data streams provide paths to the respective entity and require a category to be assigned, either profile, engagement, or other. As a result, a single data source can contain multiple data streams.

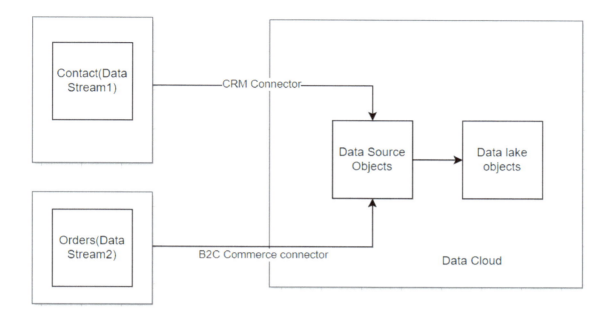

Above diagram shows two source systems. Each source system has 1 data stream. Arrows show connectors for each source system. And Data can be viewed from Data lake objects.

A data stream has two modes-:

Upsert Mode-:

- When your data stream is created in upsert mode, for each refresh, if there's new data, it's added, and if there's an update to existing data, it's updated. Full Refresh o

Full Refresh mode-

- When your data stream is created in full refresh mode, during each refresh cycle, all existing data is deleted and replaced with the newly imported dataset.

Suppose a new field is added to the source system and we need to map this field to data cloud. We must ensure that the integration user on source system should have access to this new field.

Suppose a customer uploads new customer data to an Amazon S3 Bucket on daily basis to be ingested in data cloud. Identity resolution, segmentation and calculation insights should run on refreshed data stream.

Creating a Data Stream

After Connector is configured, then Data Stream should be created.

To create a Data Stream, Go to **Data Streams** tab and Click on New. The raw data records that are ingested into data Cloud can be viewed from **Data Lake Objects** tab.

Second step is to Select the Connector. Below screenshot shows some connectors. MuleSoft Connectors can also be used to get data from the Source system (legacy, etc.). Connectors appear in the below window they are configured in Data cloud setup.

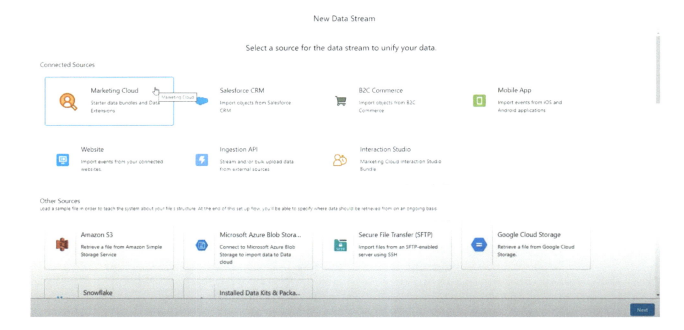

Once the connector is selected, next step is to Select the Objects/Entities and fields for a Data Stream. Additionally, category should be selected that best describes the type of object/Entity. There are three categories available-:Profile, Engagement, Other.

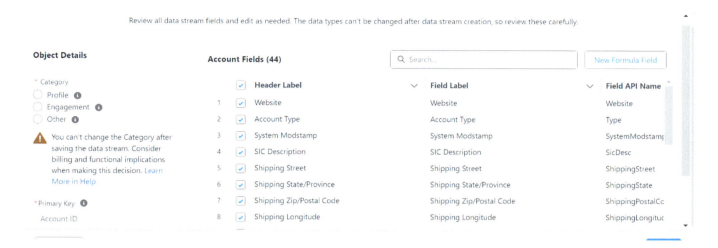

The three data categories are: Profile, Engagement, and Other.

Select **Profile Category** if your dataset corresponds to-:

- A list of consumers with identifiers such as consumer IDs, email addresses, or phone numbers

- A list of businesses or accounts with account IDs

- A list of employees or any other population that you wish to segment by, or use as the segment's starting population .

- Some examples of Profile Data are Customer or user info, their emails, phone numbers, gender, birthdate, device type, identification Id(passport).

Engagement Category

Engagement category should be selected for dataset if your dataset is time-series oriented. When you set the dataset category to Engagement, you must define the event time using a date field from your schema. When you select engagement data, the Event Time Field drop-down appears in the UI.

Here is an example of Engagement data, illustrating user engagement and their interaction with the timeline on the X-axis.

When selecting Engagement as a category in Data stream , dataset must contain **date** field. This timefield can help in identifying engagement of party at different point of time.

In future chapters we will see how **Event Time Field** can be used for segmentation of Engagement data When mapping Engagement data from a source system to Data model objects(DMO's) then primary key and Event Time field must be mapped. Engagement Data consists of following type of data-: number of clicks, downloads, opens, comments, orders and other data that shows how the user is interacting with the platform or website.

If profile or Engagement category are not suitable, then Other Category can be used.

Example of dataset for Other Category is Pricebook,Catalog.

Please note that Category of a Data stream cannot be changed after saving.

Starter bundle

Starter bundles are ready-made solutions for connecting a source system, which can save some time. Starter bundles are available in the Data Cloud. These bundles contain stream, DLO and mapping to Data Model Object.

According to Salesforce documentation, below is definition of Starter Bundle:

A starter data bundle is a Salesforce-defined data stream definition that includes mapping to Data Cloud DMOs. After a data stream is deployed, the starter data bundle automatically maps source objects from the source to a DMO in Data Cloud. You can add or customize the data mappings to meet your business needs.

When we use Starter Bundle for Marketing Cloud, the following data sets are readily available and mapping for these data sets is also included. There is no need to map the fields to DMO manually.

Below is example of Starter Bundle: If you install the "Marketing Cloud Engagement: Contact Mappings" starter pack in your Data Cloud org, the following mapping is included as part of the starter pack:

SFMC Contact Point App Data Stream

DLO Field	DLO Field Data Type	DMO	DMO Field	Additional Info
Application ID	text	Contact Point App	Software Application	
Badge Count	number	Contact Point App	Badge Count	
Device ID	text	Contact Point App	Device	
		Device	Device ID Primary Key	
Device Name	text	Device	Name	
Device Type	text	Contact Point App	Asset Type Id	
Id Primary Key	text	Contact Point App	Contact Point App Id	Primary Key
		Party Identification	Party Identification Id	Primary Key
OS Name	text	Device	OS Name	
OS Version Number	text	Device	OS Version	
Party Identification Name	text	Party Identification	Identification Name	
Party Identification Type	text	Party Identification	Party Identification Type	
Registration Id	text	Party Identification	Identification Number	

8. Data Modeling Data Cloud

Salesforce Data Cloud has a canonical data model that includes data lake objects (DLO), and data model objects (DMO).

A canon approach would mean having one customer or person with related orders and products, etc., with a set of IDs, attributes, and associations that the entire enterprise can agree upon.

A CDM is also known as a common data model because that's what we're aiming for—a common language to manage data!

Data from different Data sources is mapped to a common Data model. Canonical data model appears as bellow:

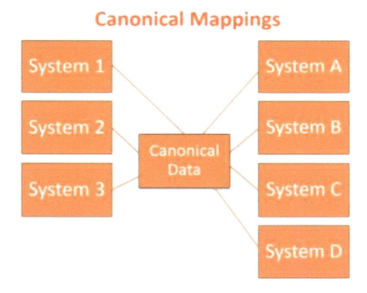

According to the definition, DMOs are defined as virtual views of a data lake objects (DLOs).

DLOs are storage containers within the data lake for the data ingested into all data streams within Data Cloud. These data lake objects are automatically created from Data Source Object. A data model object (DMO) can establish either standard or custom relationships with other DMOs. These relationships may be structured as one-to-one or many-to-one. You can view the relationships and their statuses on a DMO record's Relationships tab.

DSO (Data Stream Object) is another concept which will be defined in the last chapter, where we will discuss Ingestion and Data Streams. You will not find any tab for Data Source Object in Data Cloud. This is because under the hood Data Lake Objects is used to store the Source data. Data source objects is just temporary storage.

Two Data Model Objects can be related via following relationships:

- One to one
- Many to one

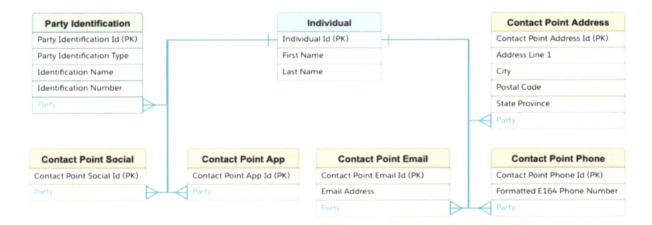

Individual is representation of a person. A single customer may possess multiple email addresses; hence, a one-to-many relationship is utilized between Individual and **Contact Point Email**. Contact Point Email can have multiple emails addresses for the same Individual. Party identification stores unique identifiers for a customer, such as a passport or driver's license.. Also note that lookup field to Individual object is called **Party**.

Let's take an example if a customer has Master Customer table (containing fields such as Name, email, personally identifiable information) from their CRM to ingest into Data Cloud, the Name field should be mapped to individual object, while the Email address should be mapped to the Contact Email object.

Standard and Custom Relationships

Standard and Custom Data Model Objects can be accessed via **Data Model** Tab

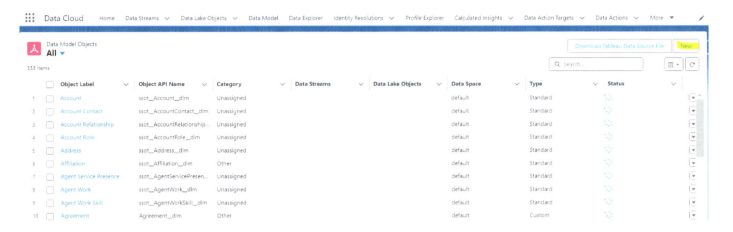

New Data model can be created using New button. Click on the Edit button to add new fields or add new relation ships-:

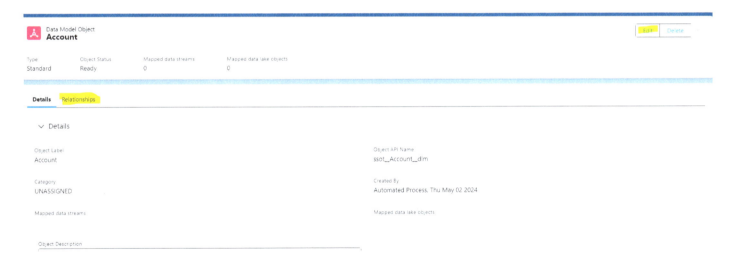

In the Data Cloud data model, there are standard relationships that become active once the related object fields are mapped. Activation occurs when there is at least one mapping for both fields. Conversely, removing a mapping for at least one field deactivates the relationship. While you can disable a standard relationship, deleting it is not an option. A standard relationship becomes visible on the Relationships tab only when activated.

Optimize DMO relationships as follows:

Instead of relating all objects to individual Object, you can categorize all Credit Cards under banking object.
As shown in the right diagram, the below diagram is from Salesforce documentation:

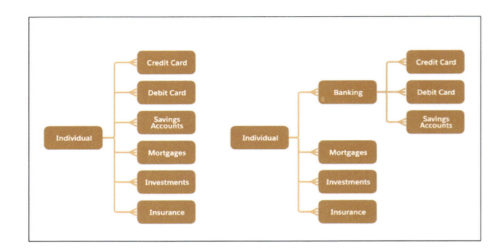

Data Spaces

According to the definition, a data space serves as a logical partition designed, to streamline the organization of your data for profile unification, insights, and marketing within the Data Cloud. This feature allows you to categorize your data, metadata, and processes into distinct groupings, such as brand, region, or department. By doing so, users can access and manage data exclusively within the context of their designated category. Additionally, data spaces facilitate the merging and analysis of data for enhanced insights and decision-making capabilities.

Unlike using multiple instances of a Data Cloud, Data Spaces provide an efficient means of managing different datasets within a single instance. This not only has the potential for cost savings but also simplifies the overall data administration process.

When a new data space is created a new permission set is added with the Name of Data space. This permission needs to be assigned to the user who needs access to the Data Space.

As of now 50 Dara Spaces can be created in Data Cloud Account

Moreover, Data Spaces prove to be valuable in aligning with Software Development Lifecycle (SDLC) processes. By establishing segregated environments within Data Spaces, organizations can conduct staging and testing of data objects without affecting live data in the production environment. This separation minimizes the risk of unintended consequences during the development and testing phases.

In summary, Data Spaces offer a flexible and efficient solution for organizing data within a single Data Cloud instance. They provide control over data access, allow for logical separation based on various criteria, and facilitate adherence to SDLC processes, making them a valuable asset for organizations managing diverse data requirements.

Below diagram is from Salesforce documentation:

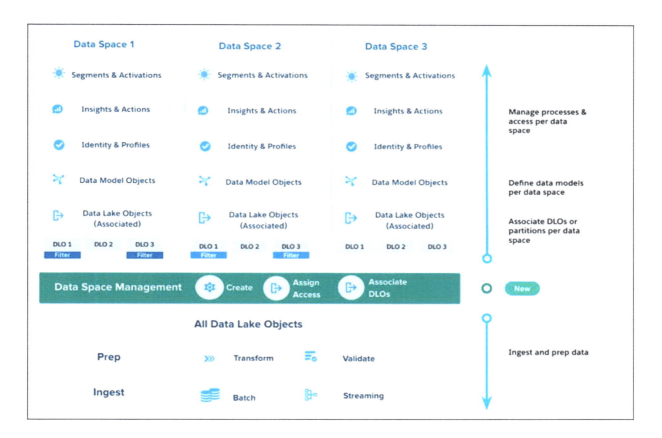

Dan Heath once said: "Data are just summaries of thousands of stories-tell few of those stories to make data meaningful".

Creation of a Data Model Object

Data model objects are fundamental building blocks of data Cloud. DSO and DLO use a physical data store. DMO offers a virtual, non-materialized view of the data in the data lake.The result from running a query associated with a view is not stored anywhere and is always based on the current data snapshot in the DLOs.

When you login into a new data Cloud organization, some standard objects (Data Model Objects) are already present. Custom fields can be added to such standard objects (DMO's). New custom objects (DMO) can also be created.

As shown in the image below, three options can be used to create a Custom DMO. After DMO is created, fields can be added to it. Selecting primary key is must. Value suggestion can be enabled for a field. Value suggestion takes up to 24 hours to reflect.

When data model object is created then Object Label, Category, and Object Description are specified. Category can be Profile, Engagement and Other.

Value suggestion is a feature of Data Cloud that allowing you to identify and select text attributes from a pick list of options. You can use value suggestion to standardize values across different data sources and improve the quality of data.

Moreover, you can enable value suggestions for data model object (DMO) fields if the data is in text form. You can enable or deactivate the feature in the DMO record home. Value suggestions can be enabled for up to 500 attributes for your entire organization. It can take up to 24 hours for suggested values to appear.

The Customer 360 Data Model organizes similar data model objects (DMOs) together into data model subject areas to help understand and use the data model.

DMOs are organized into different Data Object subject areas, including:

- **Case:** for service and support cases

- **Engagement:** for engagement with an Individual, like email engagement activity (send, open, click)

- **Loyalty:** for managing reward and recognition programs

- **Party:** for representing attributes related to an individual, like contact or account information.

- **Privacy:** to track data privacy and consent data privacy preferences for an Individual.

- **Product:** to define attributes related to products and services (goods)

- **Sales Order:** for defining past and forecast sales by product.

9. Data mapping in Data Cloud (between Data lake Objects and Data Model Objects)

Data mapping should be done keeping the goal in mind. The goal is to act on data , based on user behavior, events, milestones, data trend, etc. Actions are always around customers. This makes the individual the important object, it has all the personal information you know about your customer.

Data Streams can be mapped to data model objects. Data Stream is also referred to as DLO (Data Lake Object) while we map data on data cloud. Data coming from source system is stored in Data Lake Objects in raw format.

To use identity resolution, all data streams with customer information must have a field mapped to the individual ID field from the individual object.

If we are getting Contact Object data from Sales Cloud. This data will be stored in Data lake object. Data Model Object and field mapping is automatically created for the source. Mapping can be edited if required.

In below case -:

- Company related data will be mapped to Account,
- Person related data like name, birthdate will be mapped in Individual and
- Email will be Contact Point email
- Phone will be mapped to Contact Point Phone
- Any Passport will be mapped to Party Identifier.

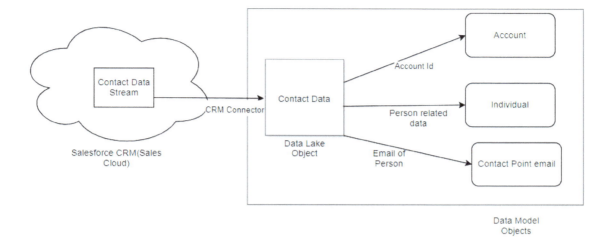

To start mapping go to Data stream Tab and Click on Start in the Data Mapping section.

The Data Stream (Data Lake objects) is mapped to the Data Model Object in the data cloud.

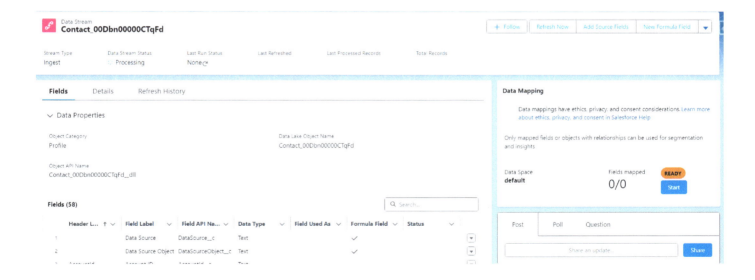

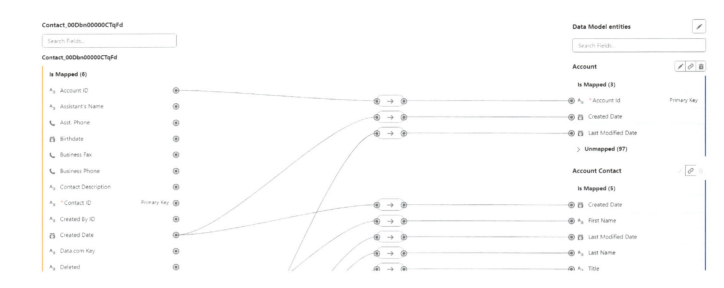

Below are some helpful links for Data mapping-

:https://trailhead.salesforce.com/content/learn/modules/data-and-identity-in-salesforce-cdp/maprequired-objects

https://help.salesforce.com/s/articleView?id=sf.c360_a_data_mapping_best_practices.htm&type=5

Best practices while mapping data in data cloud:

1. It is a good practice to create data dictionary for source system. A data dictionary is a structured repository of metadata that provides a comprehensive description of the data used.

2. Understand how each source object relates to Individual Object (Party or Customer or End User). Understand what primary key for Source system is. And if you are combining data from multiple sources, what is type of data coming from each source and their Primary key. For example, if you're bringing in web engagement data, ensure that it's mapped to the Individual DMO or an attribute that is mapped to the Individual DMO to better understand user consumption and behavior on your site.

   Data is stored in a data cloud in a normalized format to reduce redundancy, while data from inconsistent sources needs to be transformed and mapped to the Salesforce tables below:

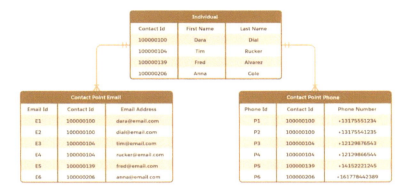

3. Data Model Object (DMO) inherits its category from the first DLO mapped to it. After the DMO inherits a category, only data source objects with the same category can map to it.

   • You can map a DLO to one or more DMOs.
   • You can map only one DLO field to a DMO field. A single DMO field cannot have more than one source DLO field.
   • You can map a DLO field to more than one DMO field in the same DMO.
   • Engagement DLOs can map only to Engagement DMOs.

4. Primary key of Data Lake object must be mapped to Data Model object.

   • If field is not available field can be created on the fly

5. Data can be mapped with Data Model Object of the same Data space.

When we cannot remove data model mappings:

   • When the field mapping referential integrity check fails. The Customer Data Platform performs a referential integrity check when you try to remove a field mapping. If the referential integrity check fails, you can't remove the field mapping. If you want to change the field mapping from one DLO field to another field in the same DLO, the referential integrity check also prevents you from changing the mapping. To circumvent this check, you can set up a temporary field mapping to a different DLO.

- When the field mapping that you're trying to remove is used in a Customer Data Platform FlexiPage.

- Delete Object is not available if the DMO has downstream dependencies, such as Identity Resolution, Segments, Calculated Insights, and Activations. You must remove the dependencies before you can delete the object.

- When at least one of the fields in the DMO has a mapping from just one DLO. When you remove that field mapping, the DMO field has no more field mappings. Because a custom DMO cannot exist without field mappings, the only valid option is to delete the DMO.

10.   Calculated and streaming insights

Calculated insights are used to query and create complex calculations based on stored data. Below are some of the examples:

- At least 5 email views per month

- Cart value over $750

- Customer rank less than 10

- Total purchase amount greater than $2000

- Open tickets greater than 1 this past year

Calculation insights can be used to narrow down results for a segment. For example, if a segment references too Many Data Lake Objects. Calculation insight can be created to reduce the complexity of a segment. Filters are available while creating a segment. However, calculation insights are used when the logic is complex.

Someone who knows SQL can easily create Calculated Insights.

As defined in Salesforce documentation, Calculated Insights allow you to define and calculate multidimensional metrics on your entire digital state in Data Cloud. Scheduling a calculated insight to process in Salesforce Data Cloud can offer several benefits for organizations looking to leverage their data effectively.

Calculated Insights can be run manually or can be scheduled. Here are a few reasons why you might want to schedule such insights:

- Timely Decision-Making: Insights are often most valuable when they are up-to-date and relevant. By scheduling insights, you can ensure that decision-makers have access to the latest information when making strategic choices.
- Consistency: Insights may need to be refreshed only when certain data streams are refreshed or only after identity resolution is complete.

- Optimal Resource Utilization: Scheduling allows you to allocate resources efficiently. You can plan the processing during off-peak hours or when system usage is lower, preventing any negative impact on system performance.
- Real-Time Monitoring: Some insights might be required more frequently, such as real-time monitoring of specific data points. Scheduling ensures that these insights are generated at the necessary intervals. Streaming insights can also be used in for usecases where Real time monitoring is required.

Calculated Insights can be scheduled using visual flow. Visual flow can be built on calculated insight(calculated insight is an object). Let us see this example to understand when flow should be used. Suppose data cloud receives nightly feed of all transactions from previous day from an ecommerce website. The result of Segmentation and activation depend on calculation insight. ,Therefore flow trigger can be used to refresh calculation insight and segment before activations are scheduled to run.

As the name implies Measure is something that is being measured in calculated insight, Dimension is the attribute used to Group by in query.

Calculated insight template:

SELECT <Attributes>, <Aggregation [_Measures_]>

FROM <Data Model Object>

JOIN [Inner | Left | Right | Full] <Data Model Object> [Optional]

WHERE <predicate on rows> [Optional]

GROUP BY <columns [_Dimensions_]> Below examples are taken from

GIT hub: **https://github.com/salesforce-marketingcloud/cdp-**

calculated-insights

Example 1:

This query helps in calculating customer spend per customer.

Individual record ID which is the customer ID is the Primary Key.

```
                                                                      total amount
                                                                      spend per
                                                                      customer
SELECT
    SUM(SALESORDER__dlm.grand_total_amount__c) as customer_spend__c,
    Individual__dlm.Id__c as custid__c
FROM
    SALESORDER__dlm
JOIN
    Individual__dlm
ON
    SALESORDER__dlm.partyid__c = Individual__dlm.Id__c
GROUP BY
custid__c
                            total amount spend is
                            calculated per customer
```

Measure	Dimension
customer_spend__c	custid__c
(Aggregate of Amount field on SalesOrder Data model Object)	(Grouped by individual Id)

Example 2: Calculate the total amount spent per customer per product

```
SELECT
    SUM(SALESORDER__dlm.grand_total_amount__c ) as customer_spend__c,
    PRODUCT__dlm.name__c as product__c,
    Individual__dlm.Id__c as custid__c
FROM
    PRODUCT__dlm
JOIN
    SALESORDERPRODUCT__dlm
    ON
        PRODUCT__dlm.productid__c=SALESORDERPRODUCT__dlm.productid__c
JOIN
    SALESORDER__dlm
    ON
        SALESORDER__dlm.orderid__c=SALESORDERPRODUCT__dlm.orderid__c
JOIN
    Individual__dlm
    ON
        SALESORDER__dlm.partyid__c= Individual__dlm.Id__c
GROUP BY
    custid__c,
    product__c
```
aggregate of total amount spent per customer , per product

Amount spent per customer for each product

Below are steps to create an insight and various methods to create an insight: First we need to Select Data Space before creating an Insight.

1. Create with Builder(drag and drop)

2. Create from SQL

3. Create from a Package- can be deployed from one org to another .

4. Create Streaming Insights

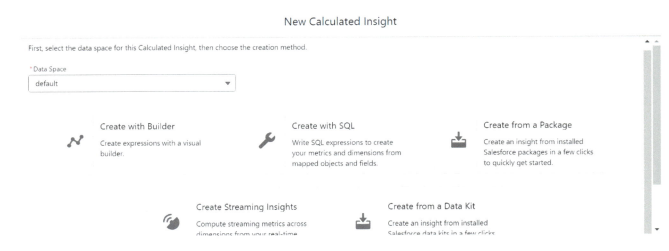

Insight Builder:

Insights can be created based on fields of Data Model Object. Functions can be used and insight can be created on top of another insight.

If you plan to use Calculated Insight in Segmentation, make sure the below conditions are satisfied:

- Include the data stream (Data model object) you segment on as a JOIN in SQL QUERY.
- The data stream (Data Model Object) primary key must also be listed as a dimension (dimension is the attribute used in Group By clause in SQL query).

The data stream (Data Model Object) primary key must also be listed as a dimension (dimension is the attribute used in Group By clause in SQL query).

Calculation insight can be used to check status of calculation insight. Data explorer tab can be used to check records processed and result of calculation insight.

New measures and dimensions can be added to an insight.

Streaming Insights:

Streaming insights are used to build complex logic on real time data. Streaming insights focus on data at a specific time. Below are some of the examples:

Data coming from a sensor

- Could also be used by support team to act upon customer responses or behavior on websites
- Another example is sending notification to users based on alert
- Create real-time Dashboards for Customer Support

A window function is a unique requirement of a Streaming Insight query. It defines the time interval for the query to run on the streaming data and the frequency of the query execution.

SELECT COUNT(RealTimeWebsiteEvents__dlm.page views__c) as page_views__c,

ssot__Individual__dlm.ssot__Id__c as customer_id__c,

RealTimeMobileEvents__dlm.product__c as product__c,

WINDOW.START as start__c,

WINDOW.END as end__c

FROM

RealTimeWebsiteEvents __dlm JOIN ssot__Individual__dlm ON

ssot__Individual__dlm.ssot__Id__c = RealTimeWebsiteEvents__dlm.deviceId__c

GROUP BY

Window (RealTimeMobileEvents__dlm.dateTime__c ,'5 MINUTE'), customer_id__c

Above example is taken from Saleforce documentation.

https://help.salesforce.com/s/articleView?id=sf.c360_a_create_streaming_insight.htm&type=5

Streaming insight can be helpful in below scenario-:

If a company wants to identify candidates, who have browsed the jobs page on their website at least three times within the last 24 hours. This data can be used in segmentation as well.

The basic requirements of an insight are data sources, measures, and dimensions (how you group the data).

Calculated insight and Streaming Insight Comparison

	Calculated Insight	Streaming Insight
Frequency	Calculated in every 6,12,or 12 hours.	Calculated in near real time.
Type of Data	Created on any type of data	Created only on Engagement data
Supported for which features	Segmentation, Activation,enrichment ,Data Actions	Data Actions
Volume of data	High Volume Bulk Data	Micro batches of real time data

11. Segmentation in Data Cloud

Segmentation helps to break down data in Data Cloud into useful segments to understand, target, and analyze your customers. Salesforce Data Cloud offers this utility to create targeted audience segments for marketing campaigns and to drive relevant experiences for customers. Segment is created on Data Model Objects (DMO).

Data flow is as follows:

Ingestion of data from Source data->Mapping Source Data to Data Model Object->Unifying data->Calculation insight->Segmentation->Activation

Segmentation is typically done at the end of the data flow in the Data Cloud, after connecting to the source, ingesting data from the source system, harmonizing, and unifying the data and creating calculation insights.

Segmentation is used find the customers with specific characteristics or behavioral patterns and act upon the data by sending data to target systems such as AWS, S3, Marketing Cloud etc.)

The first step in the creation of the segment is to choose the Data Space, and the DMO to segment on. You can only select on the dropdown list those DMOs whose category is Profile.

The second step is to select the publish type. There are two options:

- Standard Publish: You can set a schedule of 12 or 24 hours
- Rapid Publish: You can set a schedule of 1 or 4 hours

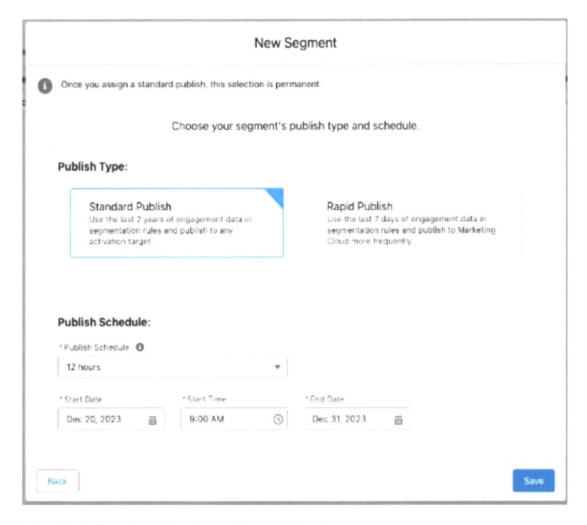

Publish schedule defines how often data will be published to target system

- Rapid schedule is only used with marketing cloud.

- The standard publish schedule is 12 or 24 hours.

- Publishing of a segment may be deferred based on publish concurrency limit.

- The time it would take to publish depends on target system.

- With Rapid publish; you can publish segments more frequently to the Marketing Cloud, considering engagement data from the last 7 days.

- Standard Publish allows for a look back of up to 2 years of engagement data and can be utilized with any activation type.

- After you create a segment, you cannot change a standard schedule to a rapid schedule, however the other way round is possible.

- Publish History can be used to check when the Segment was published.

Segment can be created through the Segment Builder or via API. Segments can be managed from external system via Segment API.

Below diagram shows how segmentation canvas is used:

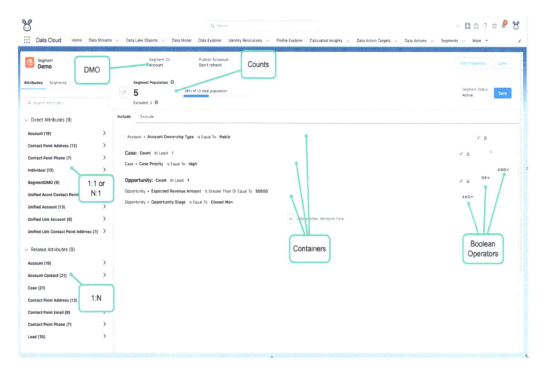

Now let me explain the above diagram.

Segment is created based on a DMO (Data Model Object). Generally segmentation is done on those DMOs that are created by identity resolution process such as Unified Individual while individual becomes a Unified Individual after identity resolution.

Population as per Salesforce documentation :

1. Total Population: Overall set of entities available in the segment.
2. Included Population: Total number of entities that qualified for you include criteria minus the entities that qualified for the exclude criteria.
3. Excluded Population: Total number of entities that qualified for your exclude criteria within the segment entities.

Under Attributes on the left there are two sections. Attributes can be dragged onto the segmentation canvas.

Direct Attributes: Shows attributes or fields of the DMO that is segmented. Also shows parent DMO attributes/fields.

Related Attributes: This shows attributes/fields of the child DMO.

Calculated Insights: Calculation Insights are built using SQL statement. A calculation insight can be added to the segmentation canvas while it will be available under the object which is referenced in SQL. It will also be available with other fields/attributes of that object; however, only processed calculation insights will be available in Segmentation canvas.

Container

Filters can be used on Segmentation Canvas to specify criteria. When a filter is defined using a related attribute, a container is created on the canvas with options to define the rules that you need. You can include up to 20 filters within a container.

For creating filters on a related DMO, it is important to check if multiple containers are required for related DMO or filters can be combined in a single container.

Example1:

Below example shows two containers on product object:

Individuals who purchased at least one of any pink product or purchased at least 1 dress:

> Products |Count| At least | 1
>
> Color| is Equal To| Pink
>
> **And**
>
> Products |Count|At least|1
>
> Product category |equals|Formal

Below example shows two containers:

Individuals who purchased Pink product and type should be Dress

> Products |count| At least | 1
>
> Color|is Equal To| Pink
> Product category |equals|Formal

For conditions added in same container the query engine uses AND logic.

Below are examples of filter that can be added to container:

1. Aggregation
2. Operators
3. Value
4. Logic

Below table is from Salesforce documentation:

Type	Description	Example
Count	Segmented based on how many times the criteria must be met	• At least 5 purchases • No more than 2 complaints
Sum	Segmented based on a chosen attribute to be summed across all data values	• Lifetime purchase value of $1500
Average	Segmented based on a chosen attribute to be averaged across all data values	• Individual average lifetime value of $500 • Customer satisfaction average of 3.5
Max	Segmented based on the chosen maximum of a specific attribute.	• Maximum purchase amount < $1000
Min	Segmented based on the chosen minimum of a specific attribute	• Minimum purchase amount > $5

Ype	Options	Use Case

Date	• Is Anniversary Of	To set up a batch email that sends to profiles on their
	• Is Not Anniversary Of	birthday, you might use:
	• Is On	
	• Is Before	
	• Is After	
	• Is Between	**Attribute**: Birth date
	• Last Year • This Year	
		Operator: Is anniversary of
	• Next Year	
	• Last Number Of Days	**Value**: Today's date
	• Next Number Of Days	
	• Last Number Of Months	
	• Next Number Of Months	
	• Day Of Week	

Type	Description	Example
	• Day Of Month	
	• Not Day Of Month	
	• Before Day Of Month	
	• After Day Of Month	

Numeric	• No Value	You want to use an attribute like total purchase amount to create a segment. The segment can be used to send a special email offer to customers who spend more than $100.
	• Is Equal To	
	• Is Not Equal To	
	• Is Less Than	
	• Is Less Than Or Equal To	**Attribute**: Grand Total Amount
	• Is Greater Than	
	• Is Greater Than Or Equal To	**Operator**: Is Greater Than
	• Is Between	**Value**: 100
	• Is Not Between	
Alphabetic	• Is Equal To	You want to send an email to customers who live in a certain state
	• Is Not Equal To	
	• Contains	
	• Does Not Contain	**Attribute**: State
	• Begins With	
	• Exists As A Whole Word	**Operator**: Is in (which allows for comma separated values)
	• Is In	**Value**: IN, Indiana
	• Is Not In	

Values

Values are actual values and logical operators are AND, OR

Let us take an example: Id segment has to be created daily for bday segment that has to be evaluated daily, than is anniversary of is a suitable operator.

If segment has be built based on customers who have visited the store in last 7 days, then last number of days operator can be used.

Empty values in data cloud can have significant impact on segment filters. If empty string comes from stream and is Mapped Data Model Object, it is stored as an empty string. If the source field is not mapped, it is stored as null.

Fields with null value will not meet the condition Is Not Equal To a value.

Link for Segmentation fiters-:

https://help.salesforce.com/s/articleView?id=sf.c360_a_examples_of_segmentation_filters.htm&type= 5

Segmentation errors from Salesforce documentation. They also show best practices when creating segments.

https://help.salesforce.com/s/articleView?id=sf.c360_a_segmentation_troubleshooting.htm&type=5

ERROR	TROUBLESHOOTING SUGGESTIONS
Segment references too many data lake objects (DLOs).	Use Calculated Insight (CI) to reduce the number of DLOs, referenced by your segment
	Split a segment into multiple smaller segments

Segment is too complex	Use a CI instead of many attributes and nested operators

	Use a CI instead of an attribute (data model Object) with many relationships
	Combine text values into one are in text operator.

Segment returns skewed data	Remove placeholder values like 0 or unknown from the source data before ingesting data into the Data Cloud

Segment is inactive	Copy the inactive segment to create a segment with the same population
Too many segments are trying to publish at the same time	Wait for some segments to finish publishing and try again

	Change the publish schedule for some of your segments
Segment population recount in progress	Wait for the recount to finish and try publishing the segment again

Segment wasn't processed	Contact Salesforce Customer Support for help
Multiple population counts are in progress	Wait for the counts to complete and try again

	Improve the segment by making it simpler, using nested segments, or merging the containers, if possible

Segment population count failed	Identify containers with the same join paths and merge them using nested operators, if possible
	Avoid long paths and use the shortest join path to reach the needed attribute

	Avoid cyclic paths in segments Cyclic paths are relationships that use cyclic behavior (a→b→a) while segment counts can fail, segment jobs can run successfully

Harmonizing and unifying data

This is the most important feature in Data Cloud.

Identity resolution is defined as the process of integrating identifiers across available touch points and devices with behavior, transaction, and contextual information into a cohesive and addressable consumer profile for marketing analysis, orchestration, and delivery.

Advantages of identity resolution are:

- Improved marketing efficiency
- Reduction in customer acquisition costs
- Better data for decision making

In a company there can be different source systems such as CRM application, marketing application commerce application, inventory application, order shipping application, analytics and mobile application for employees and customers. Suppose there are 30 source systems while each system has its own set of customers and related data and unique IDs, the data is distributed, if data can be consolidated from all source systems to make more sense. Moreover, Data Cloud has match rules and according to Salesforce documentation match rules tell Data Cloud which profiles to unify during the identity resolution process, while match rule contains one or more criteria. Moreover profiles are matched when all criteria within a match rule are satisfied. When matching accounts, these are needed: Account, Contact Point Address, Contact Point Phone, Contact Point Email, and Party Identification. Once published for the first time, your account creates unified individual profiles within 24 hours based on the rules assigned. After the initial creation, any changes made to your rules are processed on a daily basis.

After data is reconciled from different sources, the data looks like as shown below:

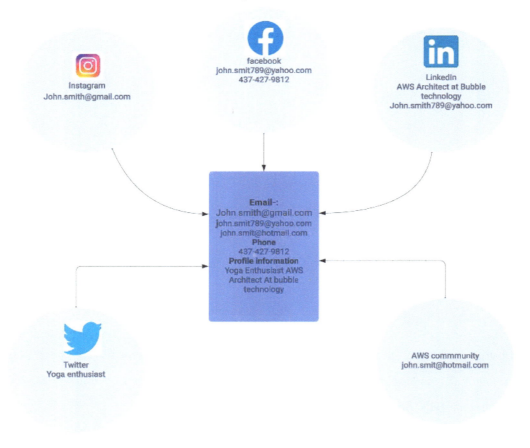

All data streams with customer information need to have a field mapped to the individual ID field from the individual object to use identity resolution

If identity resolution rule-set is deleted then following might be the impact:

Unified data associated with the rule-set will be deleted

Dependencies on Data model objects will be removed

If identity resolution rules are not working as expected the following tips can be used to troubleshoot:

Check if criteria are strict enough, if a new rule-set is created, it should be tested well before migrating to the new rule-set

Results of the old rule-set and new rule-set can be compared

The option for Ignore Empty Value helps in ignoring empty values when running the reconciliation rules. After identity resolutions run in the Data Cloud. Below illustration shows how data model looks like:

(Many Individuals are combined into Unified Individual (UI).Therefore, UI and the Individual has one to many relationships)

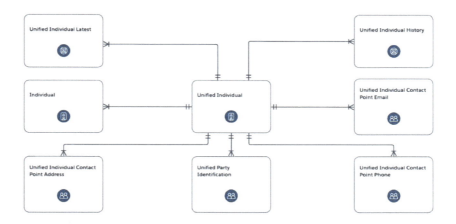

The below party identification table shows all the unique ways to identify a party (person).

Passport, Driving license are government approved ways to identify a person Suppose passport data is coming from 3 systems for a party:

IDENTIFICATION NUMBER	PARTY IDENTIFICATION		PARTY	PARTY IDENTIFICATION ID
	IDENTIFICATION NAME	TYPE		
D1469256	Canada passport	Passport	10016-0000	100
D1469256	Indian passport	Passport	10017-00001	101

For healthcare industry if identity resolution needs to be avoided while using PII data, then the patient ID can be used for data consolidation

Source priority order is used in activation to make sure data from desired source is delivered to the activation target. This is relevant when same data comes from multiple sources and one of the sources has more recent data.

Suppose the consolidation rate has increased in Data cloud, it could be due to the following reasons:

- New identity resolution rules are added which has increased the matched profiles
- New data source has been added to data cloud that overlaps with existing profiles

Consent Management and Governance in Data Cloud:

Many data protection and privacy regulations require you and your company to honor requests of people about how you use their data. We have listed a few regulations that are important to many companies in collecting and processing the data of their customers. If you have customers or users who request specific methods of contact from your company, review these common requests and the procedures related to them.

1. General Data Protection Regulation (GDPR): European Union:

   - What it is: GDPR is a set of rules created by the EU to protect the privacy and personal data of its citizens.
   - Main Points: Individuals have more control over their personal data. Companies need permission to collect and use this data, and they must ensure the data is handled securely.

2. California Consumer Privacy Act (CCPA): United States:

   - What it is: The CCPA is a law in California designed to give residents more control over their personal information held by businesses.
   - Main Points: Californians can request to see what data companies have about them, ask for it to be deleted, and opt out of their data being sold.

3. Personal Information Protection Act (PIPA), Japan:

   What it is:

- informati PIPA is a law in Japan that governs the proper handling of personal on
  Main y businesses.
- Poin ts: It outlines rules for the collection, use, and protection of personal data;
  ensuring i ndividuals are informed about how their information is used.

4. Privacy Act: Australia:

- What it is: The Privacy Act in Australia is designed to protect the personal information of the indivi luals, held by federal government agencies.
- Main ts: It regulates how agencies collect, use, and disclose personal information
  Poin and les individuals with the right to access and correct their data.
  provi

5. Personal Information Protection and Electronic Documents Act (PIPEDA): Canada:

- What it is: PIPEDA is a law of Canada that governs the collection and use of personal n by private sector organizations.

- Main Points: It requires organizations to obtain consent before collecting personal data, and individuals have the right to access their information and challenge its accuracy.

In summary, these regulations aim to ensure that individuals have more control over their personal data, companies handle information responsibly, and there are consequences for mishandling or unauthorized use of personal information. For example, a consumer asserts their right to be forgotten and requests that you delete any copies of personal data. This consumer has records in GCS and a Data Cloud profile. If you've enabled the GCS Connector, you must submit deletion jobs to both GCS and Data Cloud.

If customer has raised a request to be forgotten, it can be done in two days described below:

1. Use Consent API to suppress processing and delete the individual and related records from source data stream

2. Add the individual Id to a header less file and use the delete from file functionality

You can initiate Restriction of Processing requests for both Individual and Unified Individual profiles within the Data Cloud. It is essential to utilize the Consent API for submitting all such requests. These requests effectively limit all data processing activities related to the designated Individual and Unified Individual profiles, whereas the restriction takes effect within 24 hours.

When creating segments based on entities other than Individual and Unified Individual, it's crucial to thoughtfully consider consumer rights and expectations.

Ensure that any Restriction of Processing requests are submitted across all connected systems and Salesforce clouds. Three actions are supported by consent API:

/services/data/*vXX.X*/consent/action/processing?ids=<list_of_ids>&mode=<cdp>

If an individual exercises his right to be forgotten, then data should be deleted from Individual and related Data Model Objects in Data Cloud.

Trust based first party data asset has the following attributes:

- Provide transparency and security
- Gather data from individuals who provide consent and delete data if user does not provide the consent
- Provide value in exchange to customer(party)

John Smith requests that X Company delete his personal data. When processing his request, NTO submits a data deletion request to the Consent API, using Individual ID 1234 and 5678 in the relevant API parameters. As John requested to delete data, the below records as well as related data must be deleted, while the deletion request should be passed to the connected Salesforce clouds.

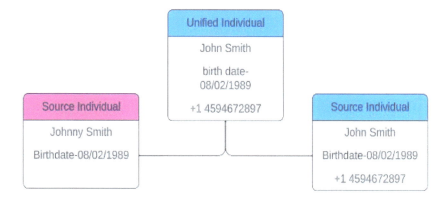

12. Activation and Data Action

Sending data to the target system is the eventual goal of Data Cloud. These golden records should be sent to the target system so that they can be actioned.

Industry experts define golden record:" Golden customer record refers to a 'single source of truth' or a 'single customer view' which consists of one unified, trusted version of data that captures all the necessary information we need to know about a customer".

Golden record that is created in data cloud as a result of Ingestion, Transformation, Data Modeling, mapping, run insights, Consolidation needs to be actioned.

Data can be sent to target in system in two ways:

1. Activation
2. Data action

Activations are used when target systems are of the following types:

- file storage
- external activation (e.g. advertising platforms) or Marketing Cloud
- Salesforce apps like Sales Cloud and Service Cloud

Activation target should be created in Data Cloud, before publishing segments to file storage activation platforms such as Amazon S3, SFTP, Google Cloud Storage (GCS), and Microsoft Azure Blob Storage.

Activation targets include a file format section so that you can export in either a CSV or JSON formatted file to a public cloud.

Data Action

Data action can be triggered on Change of Data Model Object or Calculated Insight . Action can be of three types-:

- **Webhook**: A webhook is a type of API for web applications that is event driven vs. request driven. Send data actions to any webhook target and protect the message integrity with the Salesforce-generated secret key.
- **Platform Events:** Publish platform Event from data cloud.
- **Marketing Cloud Engagement:** Send data actions to the Marketing Cloud Engagement and utilize your streaming data events to send email objects and user journeys.

Data action must be enabled before it can be used in a Data Cloud organization.

While creating a data action the following things should be kept in mind:

- Data Action Target should be created before creating a data action. Data Action target is the details about target system while checking the daily transaction limit and send notification in real time can be a good use case for streaming insight combined with data action.

Steps to Create data action-:

1. Create Data Action target (from Data Action target tab). This is the target system.
2. Create Data Action (from Data Action tab)
   a. Choose Data Action Target
   b. Choose data Space and Object type (Choose data model object or Calculated Insight)
   c. Choose Event Rule (When action should fire)

d. Action Rules(Choose condition when rule should be fired)

Marketing cloud Activation

These two steps are required when configuring Marketing Cloud activation. You need to select an activation target that represents a Marketing Cloud business unit and a contact point that represents a Marketing Cloud data extension (https://help.salesforce.com/s/articleView?)

Step1: Select a name for activation and Data Space

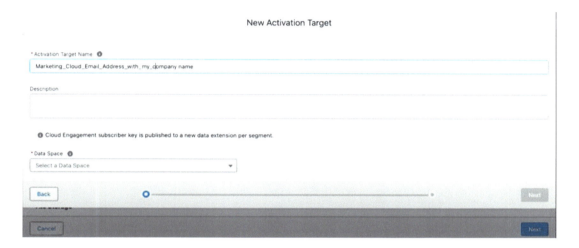

Step2-: Select a business unit for Activation-:

While ingesting data from Marketing Cloud, the Connector connects to Parent business unit . MId of parent business unit is also referred to as Enterprise Id. During activation child business unit can be specified.

Step 3: Select Segment and Activation Target

- Activation target is the target system, where segment will be published.

- Activation membership is the Entity which will be segmented. Example-Unified individual

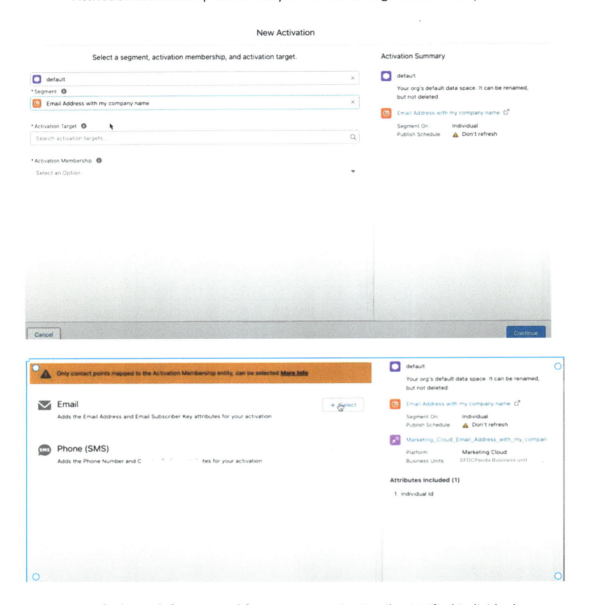

Step 4: Specify the path for traversal from Contact Point Email to Unified Individual.

There might be multiple paths choose the most optimal path.

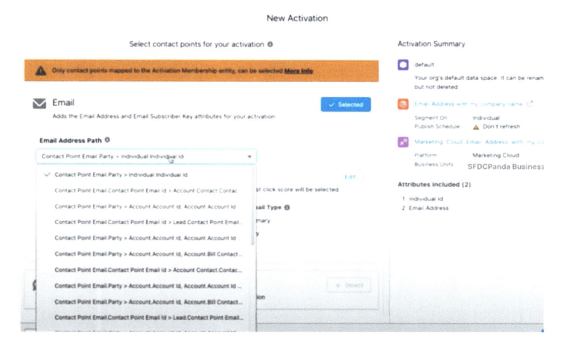

ContactPointEmail or ContactPointPhone must be specified for marketing Cloud activation.

The data streams that use the Marketing Cloud Connector (MCC) refresh data using Marketing Cloud's Automation Studio. The MCC is a feature that allows you to stream data from Marketing Cloud to the Data Cloud in near real-time. The connector uses Automation Studio to schedule and run data extracts from Marketing Cloud data extensions and send them to Data Cloud via SFTP. You can configure the frequency and time of the data extracts in Automation Studio. References: Marketing Cloud Connector

When target is marketing cloud and it has multiple BUs, the activation filters the contacts by the BUs. The segment activates as a Shared Data Extension (SDE) which can be shared by multiple BU's and not as a Data Extension (DE) to Marketing Cloud.

For some connectors activation target is automatically connected when data is ingested through these connectors. Some examples are Marketing Cloud Connector and B2C Commerce Connector.

Important point for Amazon S3 connector-:You can use the filename specification option in the Amazon S3 activation to customize the name of the file that is exported. You can also use variables such as {campaignId} to include the CRM campaign ID in the file name.

Data cloud adjusts the segmentation and activation schedules based on logged in user.

Suppose activation runs every 16 hours, data updated in source system before 16 hours are not reflected correctly in activation. To troubleshoot this-:

- Review data transformation at each level like ingestion, segmentation. Data transformation should be re-run after calculation insights.
- Ensure segment is refreshed after the data is ingested.

It is possible to get data from a separate Amazon S3 instance and send activation to another Amazon s3 instance using different credentials while configuring the stream and activation target.

Deployment

Data cloud components can be deployed to another instance by creating a package or Data Cloud kits.

A data kit is a container of Data Cloud metadata components. Data kits can be added to a package.

- When Publish is clicked, Package manager opens up.
- When a stream is added to the data kit. Associated Data model objects that are mapped to Data lake objects are also added to the Data Kit.
- Update can be used to add updated Data streams to the Data kit.

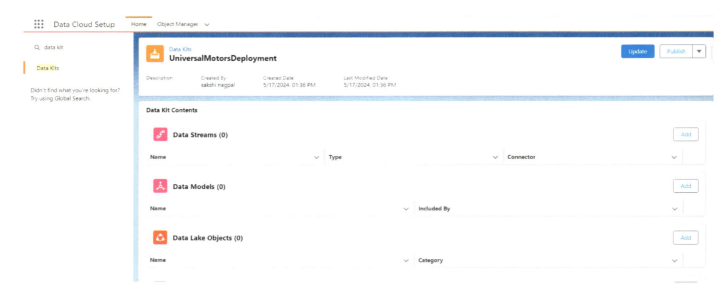

The package can be published using a package manager. Once the package is uploaded, the installation URL can be used to install the package in another organization. Segments and Identity resolution rule sets cannot be packaged.

Steps to create a package-:

1) Go to Salesforce setup and create new package Manager

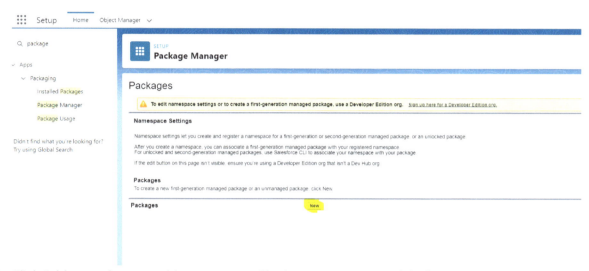

2) Click **Add to package** to add components like Stream or Data model Object.
3) Click Upload, enter version name and number and upload.

Once it is uploaded, installation URL will be generated.

13. Query API and Profile API

Profile API:

Data Cloud Profile API calls are used to look up and search customer profile information. These API calls can be included in your external web or mobile apps to look up customer profile information.

Using Data Cloud Profile API calls, you can build the complete Data Cloud Pages by retrieving the Profile info along with computed engagement insights.

Data Cloud Profile API calls follow the REST standard specification.

Use case -service Agents want to view display of all cases associated with a Unified individual on contact record. LWC and profile API are sufficient for this use case.

Query API 2.0:

Query API V2 supports SQL query in the ANSI standard. The results are returned as an array of records. The expected input when calling this API is free-form SQL. The input objects include the data stream, profile and engagement data model objects, and unified Data Model Objects. You can use Query API V2 to support a variety of use cases, which include large-volume data reads, external application integration, and interactive on-demand querying on the data lake.

API to get Data from Custom Dataspace-:

Query API can be used to get data from Data model Objects or Data Lake objects.

Authentication mechanism is different for querying data from default Dataspace and a custom Data space.

In the next chapter we will deep dive into the Authentication mechanism, for making an API call to get data from a custom Dataspace.

Below example shows how to call Query Api from postman. And the data that is being queried belongs to the default dataspace.

Firstly, we need to get access token-:

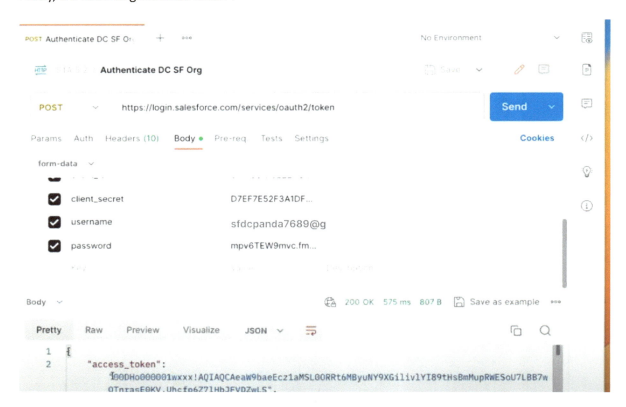

Next step is to execute query API by supplying the access token for Authentication-:

Secondly,In the header tab provide the access token-:

URL for Query API-:ssot/queryv2

SSOT is prefixed with data cloud fields and Objects and it means Single Source of truth

Thirdly provide sql(not SOQL) in the body.

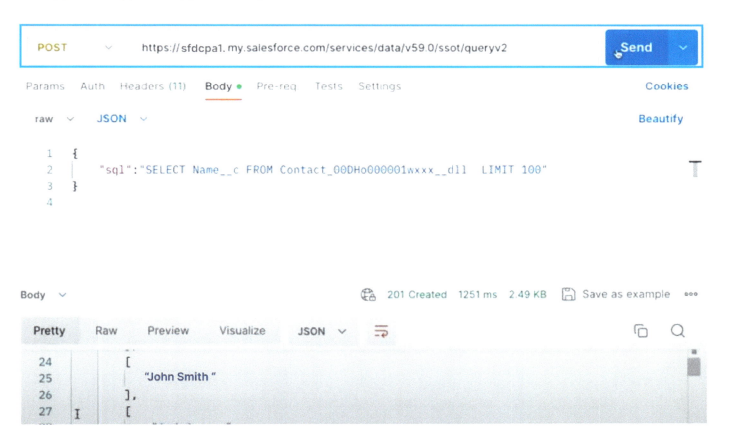

Salesforce Connect API enables you to integrate data from external sources directly into Salesforce without replicating the data. Eliminating data replication means data from external sources won't be stored physically in Salesforce.

For an instance if sensors are sending digital signal data to Data Cloud. Additionally Service Agents want to view this data to assist the Customers on a chat or a call.
For implementing this scenario LWC can be used with an apex class in the background that uses Connect API to retrieve data from Data Lake Object.

Below example shows an example how to call Connect API from Apex-:

```
@AuraEnabled(cacheable = true)
public static void getSensorData(String customerId) {
    List < Map < String, Object >> returnData = new List < Map < String, Object >> ();
    // Create input for query operation
    ConnectApi.CdpQueryInput queryInput = new ConnectApi.CdpQueryInput();
    queryInput.sql = 'SELECT * ' + 'FROM Sensor_Events_H4C06__dlm ' + 'WHERE CustomerId__c = \'' +
customerId + '\' ' + 'ORDER BY date_time__c DESC LIMIT 50';
    // Execute SQL
    ConnectApi.CdpQueryOutputV2 response = ConnectApi.CdpQuery.queryAnsiSqlV2(queryInput);
    Map < String, ConnectApi.CdpQueryMetadataItem > responseMetadata = new Map < String,
ConnectApi.CdpQueryMetadataItem > ();
    responseMetadata = response.metadata;
    // Parse response
    System.debug('Number of rows in the result data set ' + response.rowCount);
    System.debug('Next batch ID ' + response.nextBatchId);
    System.debug('Query Metadata' + responseMetadata);
    for (ConnectApi.CdpQueryV2Row resultRow: response.data) {
        for (Object result: resultRow.rowData) {
            system.debug(result);
        }
    }
}
```

Lightning page for a service agent. The component shows recent device data coming from the panels installed on the customer site. Code highlights are:

- The method takes a   customer ID   parameter, indicating that it retrieves sensor data for a

  specific customer

- An instance of ConnectApi.CdpQueryInput called Query Input is created to define the query operation

- The queryInput.sql property is set with a SQL query that selects all fields from the Solar_Panel_Events_solar_panel_H4C06__dlm data object, filtered by CustomerId__c

- The query is executed using ConnectApi.CdpQuery.queryAnsiSqlV2(queryInput), which returns a ConnectApi.CdpQueryOutputV2 object named response

14. Query API for Data belonging to Custom Dataspace

Direct API can be used to access Data Model Objects and Data Lake objects from a Custom Dataspace in data Cloud.

In this case firstly we need to request for an access token-:

- POST https://login.salesforce.com/services/oauth2/token

Secondly, we should exchange access token for a Data Cloud token-:

- POST <Instance URL>/services/a360/token
- Data space name can also be specified as Body
- Subject token is the access token(from the first call)

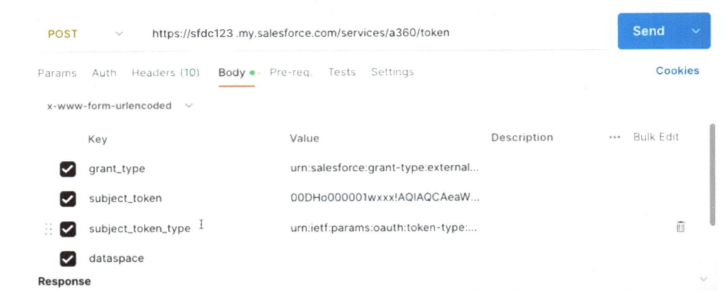

Data Cloud token that is returned in above screen is the JWT token.
Next, we should call the API by passing Data Cloud token to tenant specific URL.
Tenant Specific URL can be found on Data Cloud setup Home page-:

Are you ready to set up Data Cloud?

- ✓ Planning your Data Cloud instance.
- ✓ Creating your Data Cloud instance.
- ✓ Populating your Data Cloud instance.
- ✓ Ensuring your instance is ready.
  Your instance is located on: **CDP5-AWS-PROD1-USEAST1** ⓘ

Tenant Specific Endpoint ⓘ

gnsd1mzygnsggmjwhfsdcyrqg8.c360a.salesforce.com   📋

Last step is to make an API call to tenant specific URL.Pass the data cloud access token for authentication.
As shown below-:

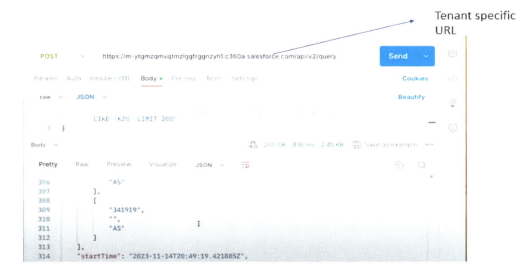

Tenant specific URL

15. Case Studies for Data Cloud

Case Study1- Clothing Case Study

Company Description: Universal Shoppers is a Merchandise company they sell clothing and other merchandises like purse belts, shoes etc. They have a lot of stores in different countries.

Problems and Pain Points for Universal Shoppers-:

- Data Distributed across various online and offline applications-:Offline data for each Store is stored in a different systems. Each franchiser(stores are owned by different people) has a different application for Managing customer data.. For Ecommerce they are using salesforce B2C Ecommerce and java website hosted on AWS platform.
- No unified view of Customer-: Customer might visit a store and visit a website soon after.
- Massive Data stored and processing in various systems-:
- Complex insights based on Unified data.
- Timeframe for Project Completion is Short.

- Some use cases that they want to achieve are as follows-:
- They wanted to unify Customer data collected from Physical Stores (Offline) and Websites(online) interactions.
- Send invite and registration link to Guest Users with Offers.
- They wanted to create complicated insights based on unified customer behavior and preferences like rfm and lifetime value-:
- Rfm- Recency,Frequency,Monetary value also known as RFM analysis, is a type of customer segmentation and behavioral targeting used to help businesses rank and segment customers based on the recency, frequency, and monetary value of a transaction.
- Lifetime Value or LTV is an estimate of the average revenue that a customer will generate throughout their lifespan as a customer.
- Additionally, they want to send Emails to users who had purchased a product yesterday from online or offline shops.

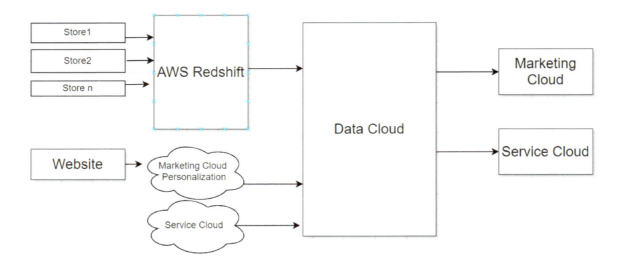

Source systems and Connectors

- AWS Redshift which is a *a data warehouse service in the cloud was used to store all the data from physical stores across all Regions.*
- For loading data from RedShift either MuleSoft connector can be used or SFTP Connector can be used along with ETL.
- *Marketing Cloud Personalization can be used to get engagement data from the Websites in near real time. And this data can be ingested into Marketing cloud via Marketing Cloud personalization Connector. It also has starter bundles.*

Data mapping-:

- Data that will be ingested into Data cloud from Source systems is stored in the Data lake obejcts.
- Data Lake objects can be mapped to Data model Objects. For Universal Shoppers Data Lake objects can be mapped to Individual, Sales Order, Email Engagement,Shopping Cart Engagement.

Insights

- Calculation Insight can be used to create insights such as RFM and LTV.

LifeTime Value

LifeTimeValue important for all businesses of all sectors. LTV is total revenue generated from a customer. If Orders indicate customer purchase then sum of all the order values can give LTV

Left join between Sales Order and Unified Individual will help in creating this calculated insight.

This data can also be grouped by Purchase channel(Facebook,instagram,website,app etc.) ,Product category, Puchase time ,etc.

Intersection of Orders and unified individual gives Life time Value-:

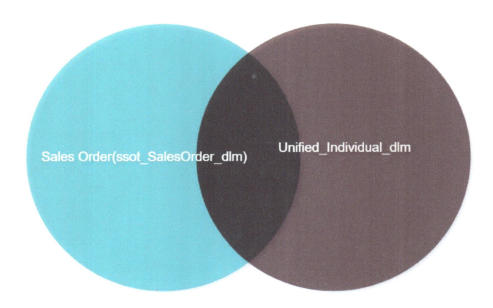

RFM-:

- RFM analysis, is a type of customer segmentation and behavioural targeting used to help businesses rank and segment customers based on the recency, frequency, and monetary value of a transaction.

- Customer data is analyzed based on most recent Purchase date, total amount spent,number of orders in the specified timeframe.Based on the analysis customer are assigned to different categories or buckets like Loyal,Promising, New,Warm,Sleepers,Lost etc.

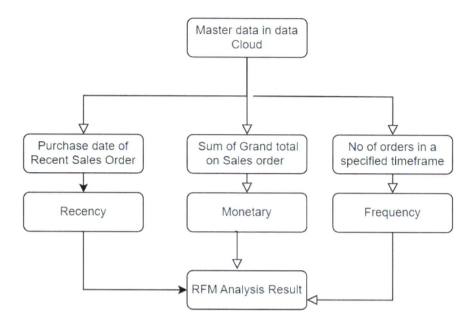

Transformations used-:

Transformation can be used to identify if any customer has purchased a Product yesterday.And sending up relevent emails for Engagement and tracking orders.

Data Action anf Activations-:

Segments can be published to Marketing cloud using standard Connectors.

Additionally, Data Distributed across various online and offline applications. Data can be ingested into data Cloud via various readily available connectors. As connectors are readily available less time and effort will be spent for Integration.

Data Cloud can store massive amount of Data, and help in consolidating online and offline data Customer profilesthrough reconciliation rules. Appropriately, Data cloud can be used by Universal Clothing to alleviate pain points and meet their goals.

Case Study 2:Royal Hotel

Pain Points and Requirements-:

- Segment data based on Booking history,loyalty status.Personalize notifications for different Segments.
- Providing tailored experiences that enhance guest satisfaction and loyalty.
- Predictive analytics for demand and Forecasting by analyzing booking history,market trends, historical data and external factors(such as events and holidays).This helps the marketing team to optimize price strategies,allocate resources effectively and anticipate peak periods for targeted marketing campaigns.
- Dynamic Pricing and Revenue Management-Dynamic pricing algorithm that adjusts room rates in real time based on factors like demand , occupancy level,competitor pricing and Guest behavior.
- Cross Channel Marketing orchestration-:Integration across various marketing channels including email,social media,website,mobile apps,offline channels(event and direct emails).The marketing

team can orchestrate co-ordinated campaigns across these channels to engage Guests with different touchpoints in their Journey(initial booking to post stay feedback)

- Customer Relationship Management-:They need centralized CRM system to manage guest interactions,preferences,feedback across multiple touchpoints.This allows marketing team to build Long term relationships with Guest by delivering personalized communication,targeted promotions and loyalty rewards based on guest preferences.

- Guest Experience Enhancement-:By Aggregating and analyzing guest feedback from Surveys, reviews and social media mentions, provide insights into Guest satisfaction level,pain points and area of improvement.The Marketing team can use this feedback to identify opportunities to enhance Guest experience, address service issue proactively and drive positive word-of-mouth marketing.

- Localized marketing campaigns-:leverage geospatial data to target potential guests in specific geographical regions or market segments with localized marketing segments. For Example, Marketing team can promote special offers or events tailored to the preferences and interests of Guests in different locations driving engagement and booking

- Partnership and Affinity Marketing-Enable Marketing team to identify strategic Partnerships and affinity groups that align with the luxury brand Image of Royal Luxury hotel. By Analyzing guest data and market trends the team can collaborate with complementary brands and organizations to offer exclusive packages,experiences or discounts that appeal to affluent travelers and drive brand affinity.

Below is landscape diagram, which involves source and target systems-:

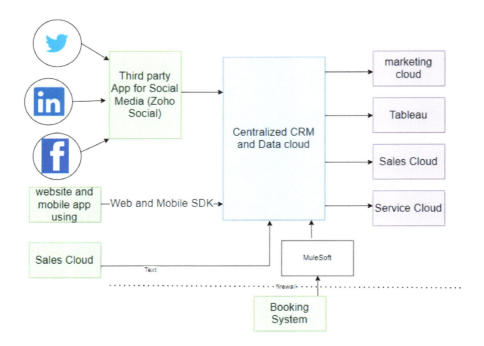

Source systems and Connectors-:

- Zoho Social or any third party apps-:This app can be used to ingest data into data Cloud when Luxury handle is mentioned on social media. Ingestion API can be used to ingest this data.
  We cannot use social studio as it is going to expire in 2024.

- Mobile App and Website-Data can be ingested from Mobile app and Website using Web and Mobile SDK.

- Booking system-Bookings and Invoices are stored in an on-premises system. MuleSoft is used as a middleware. MuleSoft fetches data from Booking system in XML transforms it and call Ingestion API. When we want to Integrate with on premise systems Mule ION's Secure Data Gateway can be installed behind the Firewall.

- Sales Cloud- Customer information is stored in the Sales Cloud. Sales Cloud is hosted on the same Organization as Data Cloud. Data can be ingested to Data Cloud using Salesforce CRM Connector. And Platform apps(on Sales Cloud) can query Data Cloud using the Connect API via REST or Apex.

- Tableau -Tableau Connector can be used to query Data Model Objects, Data Lake Objects and Calculated Insights using tableau Connector.
  - Tableau provides two modes when connecting to Data cloud live and extract mode. Live mode has its own advantages, like up-to-date data, on the other hand Extract mode tend to be much faster than live connections, especially in more complex visualizations with large data sets, filters, calculations, etc. For our usecase extract mode would be suitable. Data can be extracted per week for predictive Analysis.
  - Predictive analytics interprets an organization's historical data to make predictions about the future.
  - Data model objects like Unified individual , Engagement data and booking data can be queried in tableau for Predictions.

Segmentation and Campaigns(Offline and Online)

Once Data is Ingested into Data Cloud. Data from the Source system is stored in Data Lake Objects. Data lake Objects can be mapped to data model Objects. And reconciliation rules, can help in consolidating data. Once unification and consolidation is complete segmentation can be done.

Hotels usually attract a diverse range of guests — such as solo travellers, families, seniors, group travellers, and more.

Hotels generally have 5 market segments-:

Transient- These guests are individuals who might be travelling for business or pleasure, and who book through OTAs(Booking.com,tripadvisor,Expedia.com), travel agents or direct with hotels at non-negotiated rates.

Corporate negotiated- A corporate traveller whose business has an account (including negotiated discounts) with your hotel will fit into the 'corporate negotiated' hotel sales market segment.

Wholesale-: Wholesalers negotiate special rates with a hotel that they then resell to third-party OTAs(Booking.com,tripadvisor,Expedia.com),

Group- The group segment generally encompasses guests who are travelling as part of any sort of group (tours, corporates, organizations, religious groups, etc), and who therefore gain access to a bulk discount.

- o Segment Intelligence can be used to analyze the segments

- o Segments can be created in Data cloud based on attributes. These segments can be published to Marketing cloud using Marketing Cloud Connector. More details on configuring Marketing loud Connector are included in Activation and Data action chapter.
- o Relevant email templates and journeys can be created for each segment. For example, when guests reserve through the website booking engine, pre-arrival message can be sent to them to start planning their stay and follow up post-stay with a special return offer.

- o Real time SMS and WhatsApp communication can be sent to Customers based on bookings from the online and offline system.
- o Marketing cloud is a cross channel marketing tool which can be used to reach out to customer across various channels.
- o Segments can also be created using geospacial data for local marketing.
- o Segment Intelligence tab can be used to Analyse segment performances. It provides dashboards to analyse segment performance for different business units in marketing cloud.

Centralized CRM and data Cloud on Same Org

Data Cloud can be enabled on home org for Luxurious hotels. It would be beneficial for following use cases-

- • OOB LWC can be used to access Data cloud org.
- • Data Cloud data can be queried in Apex using Connect API
- • Service agents can use search capability on data cloud data for bookings,availability of rooms, etc.

Dynamic Pricing

A study by McKinsey says,

"dynamic pricing is the (fully or partially) automated adjustment of prices. It's a staple of the travel industry: dynamic pricing is the norm for airline tickets, hotel rooms, and ride-sharing services."

Dynamic Pricing can be implemented in various ways. Below is one optimal way of doing it-:

According to a research, Amazon changes their product prices on average every 10 minutes. This means that product prices change 144 times a day, 1008 times a week and 52.560 times a year, on average. This amount of price change is what makes Amazon the go-to space for consumers. But it also leads to Amazon being able to offer the right price at any given moment.

- Royal Luxurious Hotels wants to leverage dynamic price based on customers' buying behaviour, competitors, profit margins and inventory is used to increase profitability.
- Customer buying behavior-This can be obtained from Offline Sales people who communicate with the Customers, Website and mobile App.
- Competitor-Competitor information can be obtained from Competitor Websites, Partner and reseller websites, sales people.,Govt websites. Streaming insights can be used to get this data from source system
- Profit Margin and inventory information can be obtained from on premise booking system.

- Custom dynamic pricing engine can be built on Sales Cloud.it includes Custom components and Connect API to get Data from Data Model Objects, it can query Data lake objects via query API v2 or Direct API. And based on the Data pricing Engine can calculate the Price at regular intervals.

Survey and Feedback-Survey can be sent to Customers using Standard Surveys.Feedback can also be collected using offline forms in hotels or using third party apps on websites and mobile app. All Survey information can be fed in Data Cloud.And Insights can be created based on Survey Data. Survey Data can also be queried in Tableau for Analytics.

Einstein Engagement scores can be ingested into Data cloud via marketing cloud connector to create more insights in Data cloud. This allows for more accurate targeting, reflects real-time changes in buyer behavior, and improves ROI.

In Summary data cloud platform can empower the marketing team of Royal hotel to leverage data driven insights and advanced analytics to optimize marketing strategies,

enhance guest experiences, and drive revenue growth in the competitive luxury hotel Industry.

Case Study 3-: Create an AI model in AWS and use it for Prediction from Salesforce Data Cloud

Problem Statement for Prediction- Predict species of flower based on Sepal and Petal length.

Architecture-:

Architecture

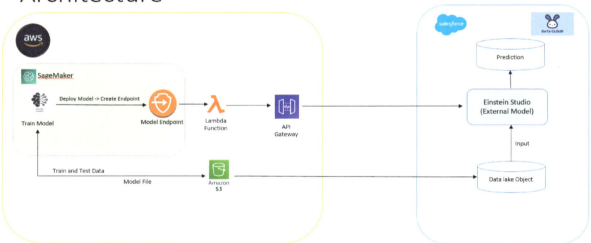

Implementation details-:

Flower related data like Sepal and petal dimensions are stored in Amazon S3. Amazon S3 connector is used to Ingest this data into Salesforce Data Cloud by creating a new Stream.

The Ingested data is stored in Data lake objects and then mapped to Data model Object.

New Model is created in Sagemaker and exposed to external systems via the API gateway.

Model can also be created using EC2 instance on AWS. In salesforce there was no options to consume the model created via EC2 instance , therefore I use Sagemaker.

In short following components were used in AWS-:

- Create a model in Sagemaker. Deploy the model and Create an Endpoint for the Model
- Use lambda to expose the model
- Use internet gateway to make the model available publically

Detailed Steps for Setup on AWS-:

I am assuming that you already have a free AWS Account. Please follow another tutorial to setup the AWS Account if required.

1. Open Sagemaker service on AWS.Create a domain, and activate it. This domain will be used for Sagemaker.We give access to users over a domain. Domain has internet access, what this means is Domain can download data from internet. Domain helps in controlling access for this Sagemaker model

In user tab add users who can access this domain.

In App configurations add the Apps that would be accessible through this domain. Apps like JupyterLab are used to create a model and train it for prediction.Below are some apps that I added.

Applications

Name	State
JupyterLab	⊘ Visible
Code Editor	⊘ Visible
Canvas	⊘ Visible
Studio Classic	⊘ Visible
RStudio	⊘ Visible
MLflow	⊘ Visible

Below is screenshot of the user tab.

QuickSetupDomain-20240913T012057

Domain details

Configure and manage the domain.

Domain settings	**User profiles**	Space management	App Configurations	Environment	Resources

User profiles Info

A user profile represents a single user within a domain. It is the main way to reference a user for the purposes of sharing, reporting, and other user-oriented features.

Q Search users			< 1 > ⚙

Name ▽	Modified on ▽	Created on ▼	
akshay	Sep 12, 2024 20:11 UTC	Sep 12, 2024 20:11 UTC	Launch ▼

1. Create S3

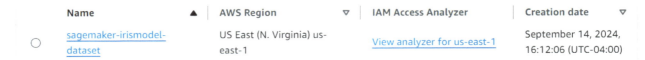

Name		AWS Region		IAM Access Analyzer		Creation date	
○	sagemaker-irismodel-dataset	US East (N. Virginia) us-east-1		View analyzer for us-east-1		September 14, 2024, 16:12:06 (UTC-04:00)	

A role in AWS can be assigned to an user or a service.

Create a Role in AWS that gives access to S3, Sagemaker, API gateway, Lambda.

Below are the policies that were added to the Role.

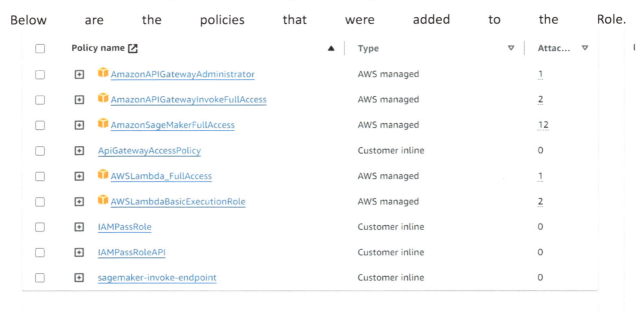

Policy name ↗		Type		Attac...
☐ ⊞ 📦	AmazonAPIGatewayAdministrator	AWS managed		1
☐ ⊞ 📦	AmazonAPIGatewayInvokeFullAccess	AWS managed		2
☐ ⊞ 📦	AmazonSageMakerFullAccess	AWS managed		12
☐ ⊞	ApiGatewayAccessPolicy	Customer inline		0
☐ ⊞ 📦	AWSLambda_FullAccess	AWS managed		1
☐ ⊞ 📦	AWSLambdaBasicExecutionRole	AWS managed		2
☐ ⊞	IAMPassRole	Customer inline		0
☐ ⊞	IAMPassRoleAPI	Customer inline		0
☐ ⊞	sagemaker-invoke-endpoint	Customer inline		0

Go to IAM service. Assign Role to to the user .I created a role named sagemaker-demo and assigned it to my user. I will use this user

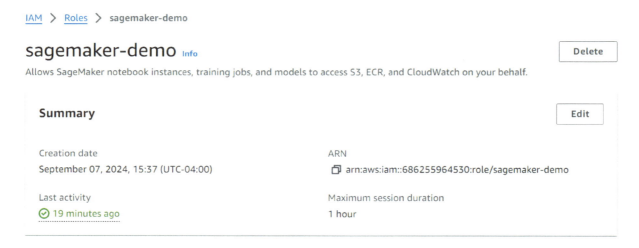

IAM > Roles > sagemaker-demo

sagemaker-demo Info   Delete

Allows SageMaker notebook instances, training jobs, and models to access S3, ECR, and CloudWatch on your behalf.

Summary   Edit

Creation date
September 07, 2024, 15:37 (UTC-04:00)

ARN
⧉ arn:aws:iam::686255964530:role/sagemaker-demo

Last activity
⊘ 19 minutes ago

Maximum session duration
1 hour

Next we will go to Amazon sagemaker to create and deploy our model.

To get started with writing the code with Amazon sagemaker, click on Title(Amazon Sagemaker) on left top. And click on Notebooks option in the left. Python code can be written and interpreted in these notebooks.

By definition Jupyter notebook is defined as- It is an interactive computational environment, in which you can combine code execution, rich text, mathematics, plots and rich media.

Create notebook instance. After use stop the notebook instance and start again when required to avoid extra costs.

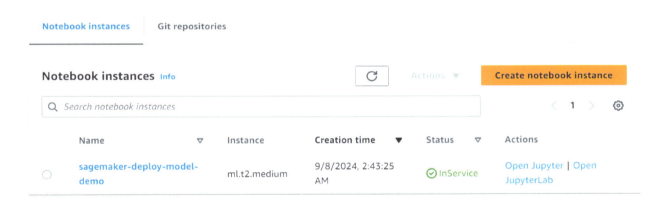

Below is detailed view of the notebook instance.

sagemaker-deploy-model-demo

Delete   Stop   Open Jupyter   Open JupyterLab

Notebook instance settings   Edit

Name
sagemaker-deploy-model-demo

Notebook instance type
ml.t2.medium

ARN
arn:aws:sagemaker:us-east-1:686255964530:notebook-
instance/sagemaker-deploy-model-demo

Elastic Inference
-

Volume Size
5GB EBS

Lifecycle configuration
-

Platform identifier
Amazon Linux 2, Jupyter Lab 3

Status

While creating the version please use the Free notebook version- ml.t2.medium.Refer aws documentation for more details. And the name of the free version might change in future.

sagemaker-deploy-model-demo

Delete   Stop   Open Jupyter   Open JupyterLab

Notebook instance settings   Edit

Name
sagemaker-deploy-model-demo

Notebook instance type
ml.t2.medium

ARN
arn:aws:sagemaker:us-east-1:686255964530:notebook-
instance/sagemaker-deploy-model-demo

Elastic Inference
-

Volume Size
5GB EBS

Lifecycle configuration
-

Platform identifier

In the permission section, Assign permissions to notebook-: We had created a role named Sagemaker - demo   earlier,   same   is   used   here.

Permissions and encryption

IAM role ARN
arn:aws:iam::686255964530:role/sagemak
er-demo ⌴

Root access
Enabled

Encryption key

After starting the notebook we will start writing the code,

Amazon SageMaker > Notebook instances > sagemaker-deploy-model-demo

sagemaker-deploy-model-demo

Delete | Stop | Open Jupyter | Open JupyterLab

Notebook instance settings   Edit

Name	Notebook instance type
sagemaker-deploy-model-demo	ml.t2.medium
ARN	Elastic Inference
arn:aws:sagemaker:us-east-1:686255964530:notebook-instance/sagemaker-deploy-model-demo	-
	Volume Size
Lifecycle configuration	5GB EBS
-	
	Platform identifier

Code-:

Block 1-this block is for importing all libraries. We can use Shift +Enter to run each block of code and see the results.

Block 2-Data that we will use totrain our model is hosted on the internet named as iris.data.It is highlighted in block 2.

Block 3 -:This code is fir reading the data from iris.csv

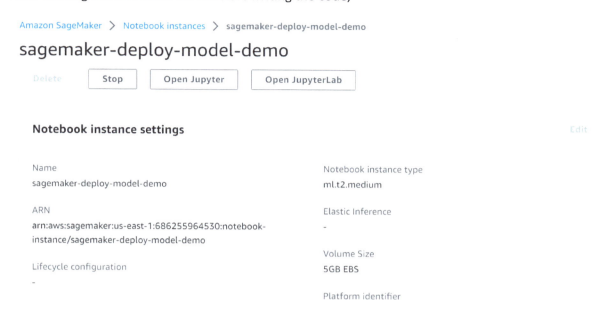

```
In [14]: import urllib
         import pandas as pd
         import numpy as np
         import seaborn as sns
         import matplotlib.pyplot as plt

In [15]: # For attributes and the class, see: https://archive.ics.uci.edu/ml/machine-learning-databases/iris/iris.names
         # For the data, see: https://archive.ics.uci.edu/ml/machine-learning-databases/iris/iris.data
         download_url = "https://archive.ics.uci.edu/ml/machine-learning-databases/iris/iris.data"
         file_name = "iris.data"
         urllib.request.urlretrieve (download_url, file_name)
Out[15]: ('iris.data', <http.client.HTTPMessage at 0x7fdfb41d2d10>)

In [3]: # Read the data into Panda dataframe
        df = pd.read_csv('./{}'.format(file_name), names=['sepal_length', 'sepal_width', 'petal_length', 'petal_width', 'species'])
```

Below code shows some observations based on data in tabular form.

```
In [5]:  # First few observations
         df.head(10)

Out[5]:
         sepal_length  sepal_width  petal_length  petal_width  species
    0         5.1          3.5          1.4          0.2    Iris-setosa
    1         4.9          3.0          1.4          0.2    Iris-setosa
    2         4.7          3.2          1.3          0.2    Iris-setosa
    3         4.6          3.1          1.5          0.2    Iris-setosa
    4         5.0          3.6          1.4          0.2    Iris-setosa
    5         5.4          3.9          1.7          0.4    Iris-setosa
    6         4.6          3.4          1.4          0.3    Iris-setosa
    7         5.0          3.4          1.5          0.2    Iris-setosa
```

Then we summarize the data based on the Attributes sepal length, sepal width ,petal length, petal width.

```
In [6]:  # Number of observations
         df.count()

Out[6]:  sepal_length    150
         sepal_width     150
         petal_length    150
         petal_width     150
         species         150
         dtype: int64
```

Below diagram shows Density plot. It shows correlation between the fields based on Attributes.

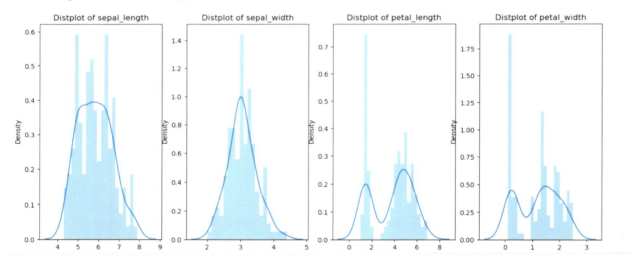

Correlation between fields

0.96 is good, The range of this value can be between 0 to 1. If Closer to 1 then correlation is positive.

In the below code we are using Heat Map to find correlation between the Attributes.

```
In [12]: # Correlation heatmap - petal length and width look to be most associated
         plt.figure(figsize=(7,4))
         sns.heatmap(df[df.columns.drop('species')].corr(),annot=True)
         plt.show()
```

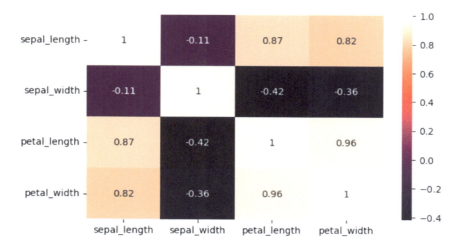

if linear relation within data, we try with linear models.

K nearest neighbour algorithm is a predictive model and linear model that be used in our case. K nearest neighbour algorithm is defined as follows-:

The k-nearest neighbors (KNN) algorithm is a non-parametric, supervised learning classifier, which uses proximity to make classifications or predictions about the grouping of an individual data point. It is one of the popular and simplest classification and regression classifiers used in machine learning today.

Below written code snippet is used to Split the data for training and testing.

Prepare the training and test data

```
In [15]: # Create training and test dataframes based on a random 70/30 split
         train_data, test_data = np.split(df.sample(frac=1, random_state=np.random.RandomState()), [int(0.7 * len(df))])

         /home/ec2-user/anaconda3/envs/python3/lib/python3.10/site-packages/numpy/core/fromnumeric.py:57: FutureWarning: 'DataFrame.swap
         axes' is deprecated and will be removed in a future version. Please use 'DataFrame.transpose' instead.
           return bound(*args, **kwds)
```

Below mentioned code is used to create a model.Our Data has 3 categories, therefore 3 neighbors are mentioned in below code.

Create a knn model using the training data

```
In [16]: from sklearn.neighbors import KNeighborsClassifier

         # Declare knn classifer; classify based on most common classification of 3 nearest neighbours
         knn = KNeighborsClassifier(n_neighbors=3)

         # Train knn model
         knn.fit(train_data[['sepal_length', 'sepal_width', 'petal_length', 'petal_width']], train_data["species"])

Out[16]:      ▼     KNeighborsClassifier        ●●

         KNeighborsClassifier(n_neighbors=3)
```

In the below code we are using Boto library

Sage maker and S3 services are declared below

Training data and testdata will be saved in S3 bucket.

Create a knn model using the training data

```python
import boto3
from datetime import datetime
import sagemaker
from sagemaker import get_execution_role
from sagemaker.serializers import CSVSerializer
from sagemaker.deserializers import JSONDeserializer
# from sagemaker.predictor import csv_serializer, json_deserializer
from sagemaker.amazon.amazon_estimator import get_image_uri

# S3 config
bucket = 'sagemaker-mlmodel-iris'
train_fname = 'iris-train.csv'
test_fname = 'iris-test.csv'
output_path = 's3://{}/output'.format(bucket)

# Save training and test data to local notebook instance (without indexes and headers)
train_data.to_csv(train_fname, index=False, header=False)
test_data.to_csv(test_fname, index=False, header=False)

# Save training and test data to S3
boto3.Session().resource('s3').Bucket(bucket).Object("{}/{}".format('train', train_fname)).upload_file(train_fname)
boto3.Session().resource('s3').Bucket(bucket).Object("{}/{}".format('test', test_fname)).upload_file(test_fname)

# Training config
job_name = 'iris-job-{}'.format(datetime.now().strftime("%Y%m%d%H%M%S"))
```

Here we are declaring the ml instance on sagemaker, to train the model

```python
# Declare knn estimator
knn = sagemaker.estimator.Estimator(get_image_uri(boto3.Session().region_name, "knn"),
                                    get_execution_role(),
                                    train_instance_count=1,
                                    train_instance_type='ml.m4.xlarge',
                                    output_path=output_path,
                                    sagemaker_session=sagemaker.Session())
```

Here we are declaring the 4 features and 3 categories that will be used to train the model-:

```python
# Set mandatory hyperparameters; classify based on most common classification of 3 nearest neighbours
knn.set_hyperparameters(predictor_type='classifier',
                        feature_dim=4,
                        k=3,
                        sample_size=len(train_data))
```

Before deploying the model on Sagemaker, we can go to Sagemaker-> inference and check that Model and Endpoint is not present, it will be generated by our code

Below code will deploy our model on sagemaker. After the deployment is complete and endpoints are generated, we can go to Sagemaker-> inference and check that Model and Endpoint are generated.

After we stop the notebook instance, then we should delete the Endpoints and the model.

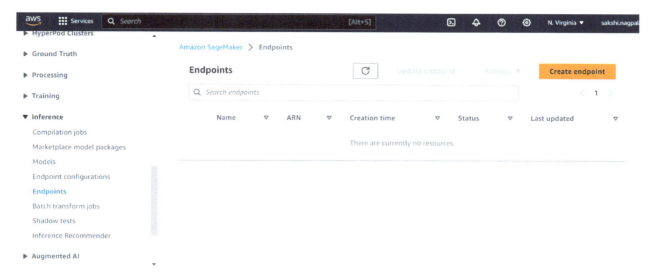

Below code is used to deploy the Model-:

Deploy the model on a SageMaker endpoint

```
In [*]: # Deploy the model to a Sagemaker endpoint
        knn_predictor = knn.deploy(initial_instance_count=1
                                ,instance_type='ml.m4.xlarge'
                                ,serializer=CSVSerializer()
                                ,deserializer=JSONDeserializer())
        # knn_predictor.serializer = csv_serializer
        # knn_predictor.deserializer = json_deserializer

        INFO:sagemaker:Creating model with name: knn-2024-09-21-13-05-28-953
        INFO:sagemaker:Creating endpoint-config with name knn-2024-09-21-13-05-28-953
        INFO:sagemaker:Creating endpoint with name knn-2024-09-21-13-05-28-953

        --
```

After creating model and Endpoint through our code

Under Sagemaker->Inference->Model we can see the new model and Endpoint created-:

▼ **Inference**

    Compilation jobs

    Marketplace model packages

    Models

    Endpoint configurations

    Endpoints

    Batch transform jobs

    Shadow tests

    Inference Recommender

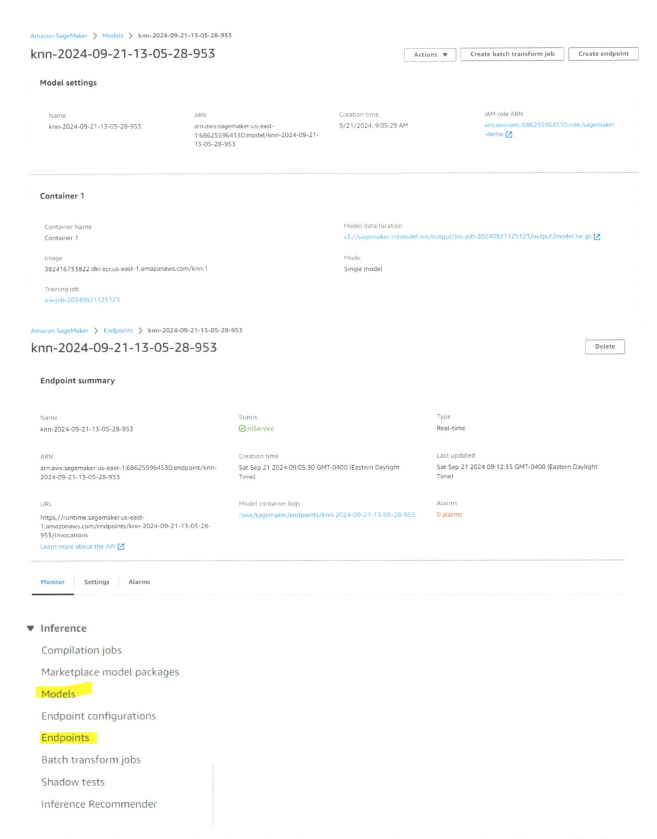

The Endpoint that is created can be used inside sagemaker only. To expose the Endpoint publically, we need a lambda service and an API gateway.

Lets go to lambda, and create a new function-:

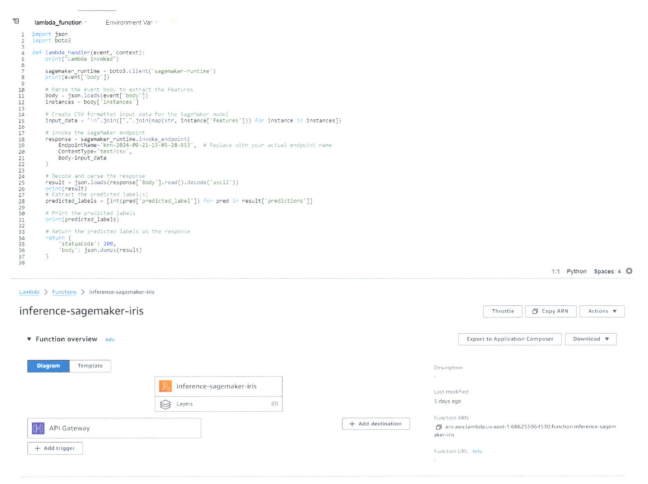

```python
import json
import boto3

def lambda_handler(event, context):
    print("Lambda invoked")

    sagemaker_runtime = boto3.client('sagemaker-runtime')
    print(event['body'])

    # Parse the event body to extract the features
    body = json.loads(event['body'])
    instances = body['instances']

    # Create CSV formatted input data for the SageMaker model
    input_data = "\n".join([",".join(map(str, instance['features'])) for instance in instances])

    # Invoke the SageMaker endpoint
    response = sagemaker_runtime.invoke_endpoint(
        EndpointName='knn-2024-09-21-13-05-28-953',  # Replace with your actual endpoint name
        ContentType='text/csv',
        Body=input_data
    )

    # Decode and parse the response
    result = json.loads(response['Body'].read().decode('ascii'))
    print(result)
    # Extract the predicted label(s)
    predicted_labels = [int(pred['predicted_label']) for pred in result['predictions']]

    # Print the predicted labels
    print(predicted_labels)

    # Return the predicted labels as the response
    return {
        'statusCode': 200,
        'body': json.dumps(result)
    }
```

1:1 Python Spaces: 4 ⚙

Lambda > Functions > inference-sagemaker-iris

inference-sagemaker-iris

Throttle   📋 Copy ARN   Actions ▼

▼ Function overview Info

Export to Application Composer   Download ▼

Diagram   Template

inference-sagemaker-iris

Layers   (0)

Description
-

Last modified
5 days ago

API Gateway

+ Add destination

Function ARN
📋 arn:aws:lambda:us-east-1:686255964530:function:inference-sagemaker-iris

+ Add trigger

Function URL Info
-

Next step is to create a new API gateway.Search for API gateway in the Global search

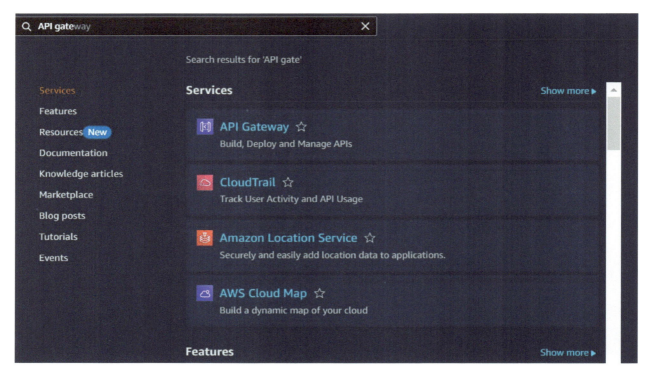

Our gateway can be called using Rest API post method, as shown in the screenshot below-:

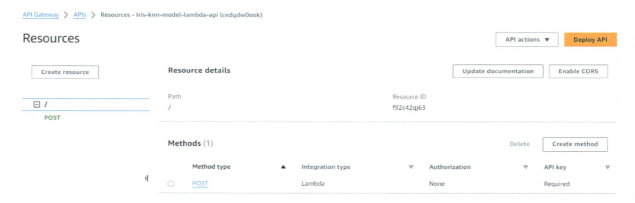

Edit method request

Method request settings

Authorization

None	▼

Request validator

None	▼

☑ API key required

Operation name - optional

GetPets

▶ **URL query string parameters**

▶ **HTTP request headers**

▶ **Request body**

Below diagram shows that request will come to the API gateway from an external system, then it will be sent to lambda. And response from lambda will be returned to the external system.

/ - POST - Method execution

Update documentation   Delete

ARN   Resource ID
arn:aws:execute-api:us-east-1:686255964530:cedqdw0ook/*/POST/   f92c42qj63

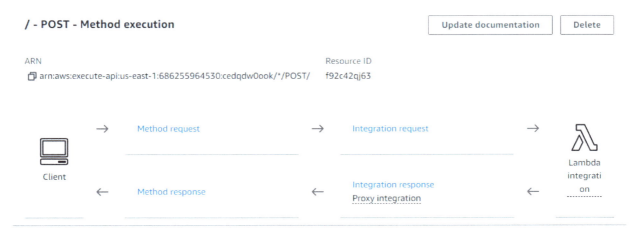

Lambda function is specified under the Integration request tab in Internet gateway-:

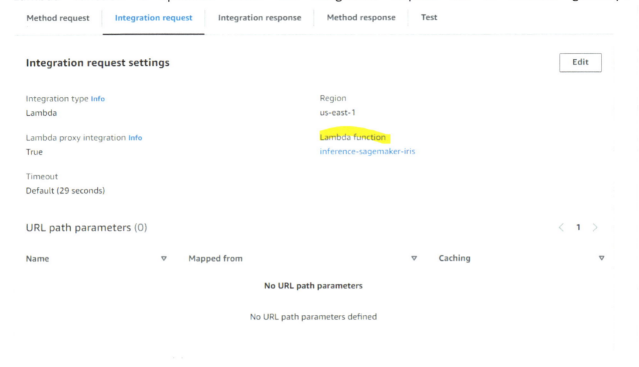

Deploy API gateway and test. Put request and test-:

Test method

Make a test call to your method. When you make a test call, API Gateway skips authorization and directly invokes your method.

Query strings

param1=value1&param2=value2

Headers

Enter a header name and value separated by a colon (:). Use a new line for each header.

header1:value1
header2:value2

Client certificate

No client certificates have been generated.

Request body

```
1 ▼ {
2       "sepal_length":4.8,
3       "sepal_width":3.0,
4       "petal_length":1.4,
5       "petal_width":0.3
6 }
```

Result for API-

/ - POST method test results

Request	Latency ms	Status
/	717	200

Response body

```
{"predicted_label": 2}
```

Response headers

```
{
  "X-Amzn-Trace-Id": "Root=1-66eeceb9-
505afba6a63c49b5867f2219;Parent=1f9646373a31445d;Sampled=0;Lineage=1:e5b88b5e:0"
}
```

Logs

Associate a usage plan with API gateway also specify lambda

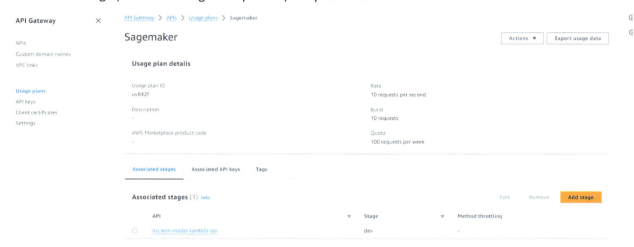

API key that is generated should be shared with external systems.

Click on the button below to Add a usage plan-:

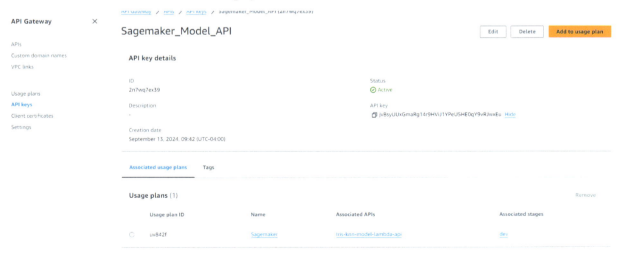

On the left menu, API Key is available. This key needs to be configured in external system for authentication.

Test method

Make a test call to your method. When you make a test call, API Gateway skips authorization and directly invokes your method.

Query strings

```
param1=value1&param2=value2
```

Headers

Enter a header name and value separated by a colon (:). Use a new line for each header.

```
header1:value1
header2:value2
```

Client certificate

No client certificates have been generated.

Request body

```
1 ▼ {
2       "sepal_length":4.8,
3       "sepal_width":3.0,
4       "petal_length":1.4,
5       "petal_width":0.3
6 }
```

The Endpoint can be found if you click on Stages in API gateway, as shown in the screen below-:

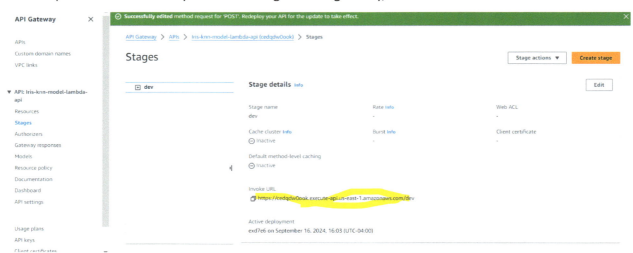

Test endpoint from postman

Specific the API key in headers-:

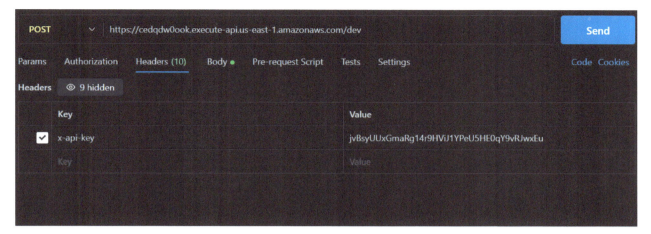

Add the request in Body, as shown below-:

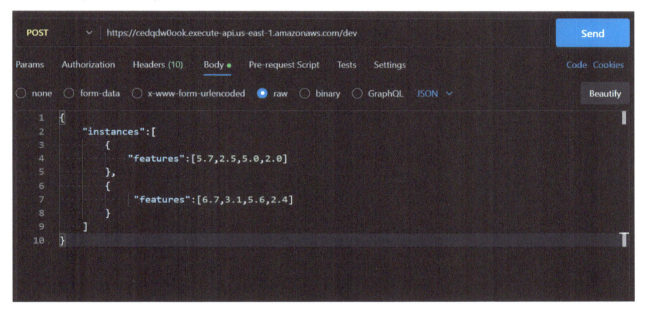

 For above Approach we could also use EC2 instance ,however if we use EC2 instance instead of Sagemaker we need to install Jupyter notebook or any other IDE,python and its libraries on the EC@ instance.Sagemaker gives 250 hours of free usage of ml.t3, as shown in screenshot below.

Amazon SageMaker capability	Free Tier usage per month for the first 2 months
Studio notebooks, and notebook instances	250 hours of ml.t3.medium instance on Studio notebooks OR 250 hours of ml.t2 medium instance or ml.t3.medium instance on notebook instances
RStudio on SageMaker	250 hours of ml.t3.medium instance on RSession app AND free ml.t3.medium instance for RStudioServerPro app
Data Wrangler	25 hours of ml.m5.4xlarge instance
Feature Store	10 million write units, 10 million read units, 25 GB storage (standard online store)
Training	50 hours of m4.xlarge or m5.xlarge instances
Amazon SageMaker with TensorBoard	300 hours of ml.r5.large instance

For our example we are using Sagemaker, Sagemaker model can be exposed in Salesforce Data cloud.

Steps in data Cloud to call Model on AWS

1. Create Connector in data Cloud

   Go to Data Cloud Setup, search for Connectors, and add a connector for S3 bucket.

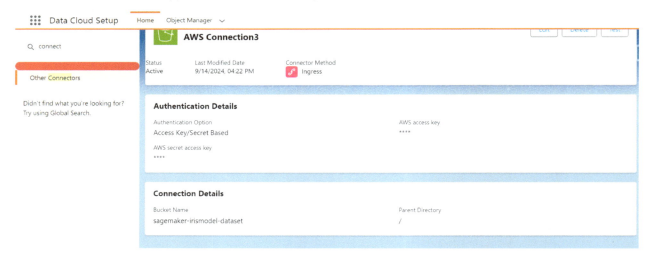

2. Go to Data Cloud app and create stream in data cloud for S3. We are creating this stream to get the test data to data cloud. We will use this data for testing our model.
   Go to Data Stream tab, and create a new Stream, select Amazon S3 Connector.
   Select the s3 bucket name, Parent Folder path and File type.
   Select the fields and the primary key for the data set-:

Once data stream is created, Data Lake Objects and data model Objects are automatically created. Data lake objects fields are automatically mapped to Data model object.

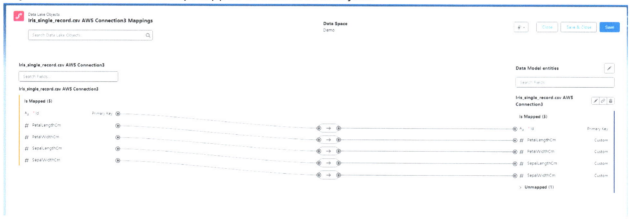

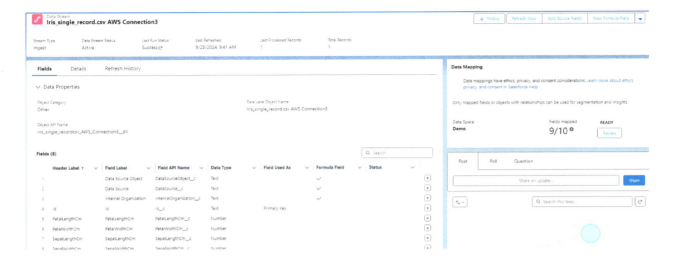

We can go to Data Model tab and created an additional field to store the predicted value that our Model on AWS will return.

Go to Data Model . Select your data model Object. And edit it to add additional field.

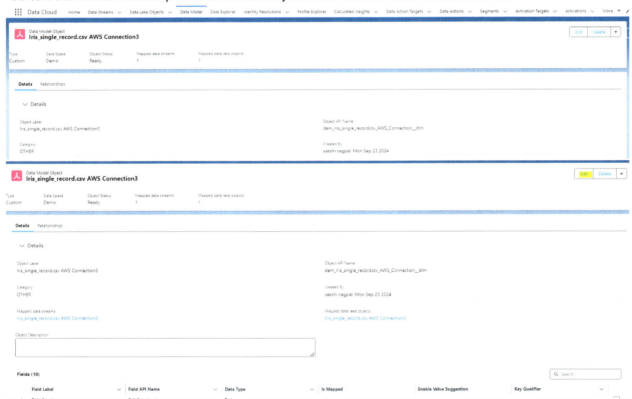

Click Add field and add the field Predicted_label

Create a AWS Sagemaker model in Data cloud in Einstein studio

Go to Einstein Studio tab. Click on Add predictive model

Select connect to an Amazon Sagemaker model

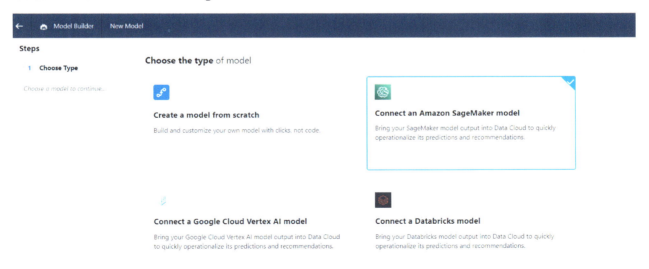

Enter a suitable name,URl(endpoint created on AWS) of the model on AWS and authentication details.

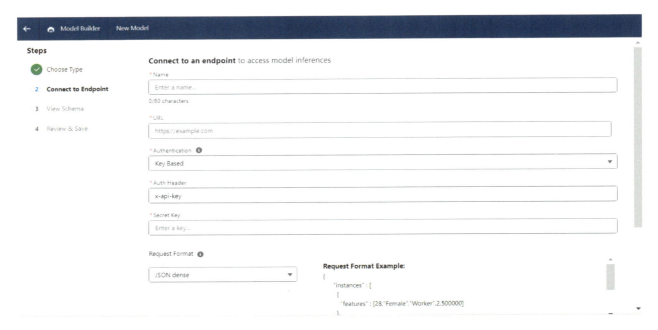

- URL can be obtained from Stages in Internet gateway,
- API key can be obtained from API key in Internet gateway

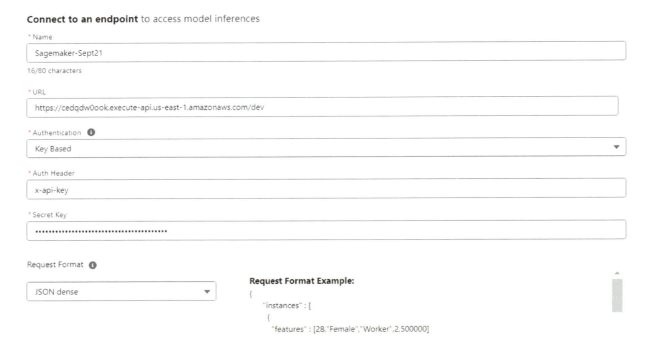

When we create this model we need to Specify the input parameters and output parameters.

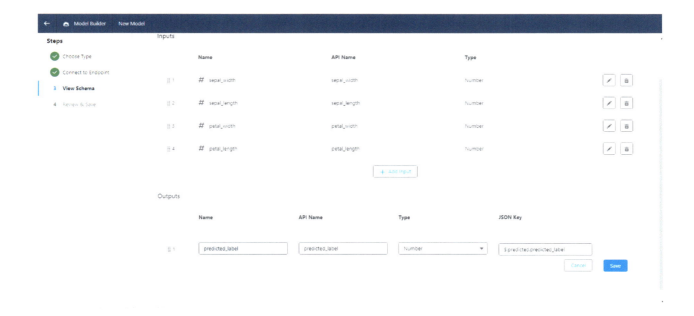

Activate the Model. Then go to Integrations tab

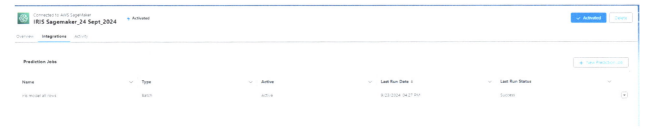

And create new prediction job. Select the Data Space, Data Model Object and map the fields.

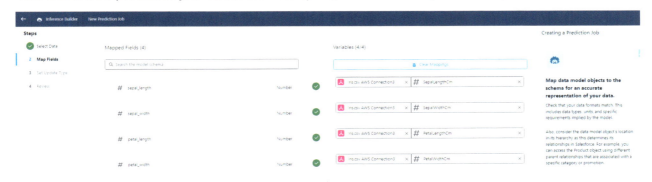

Steps for Debugging the Model-:

If the model fails in Salesforce, we cannot use salesforce debug logs for debugging this.

We can check the logs in AWS using Cloud monitor . You can see the request and response on AWS in logs.

▶	2024-09-23T19:38:52.535Z	END RequestId: 98280b20-2847-4ae4-8853-838a83391b59
▶	2024-09-23T19:38:52.535Z	REPORT RequestId: 98280b20-2847-4ae4-8853-838a83391b59 Duration: 579.96 ms Billed Duration: 580 m...
▶	2024-09-23T19:38:52.611Z	START RequestId: 9813b698-2cf0-43f2-91df-cea8fc7f5e60 Version: $LATEST
▶	2024-09-23T19:38:52.611Z	Lambda invoked
▶	2024-09-23T19:38:52.635Z	{"instances":[{"features":[5.7,2.5,5.0,2.0]},{"features":[6.7,3.1,5.6,2.4]},{"features":[5.7,4.4,...
▶	2024-09-23T19:38:53.167Z	{'predictions': [{'predicted_label': 2.0}, {'predicted_label': 2.0}, {'predicted_label': 0.0}, {'...
▶	2024-09-23T19:38:53.167Z	[2, 2, 0, 1, 0, 1, 2, 2, 0, 2, 2, 0, 1, 1, 1, 0, 2, 2, 0, 2, 2, 2, 2, 2, 2, 0, 1, 2, 1, 0, 2, 1, ...
▶	2024-09-23T19:38:53.195Z	END RequestId: 9813b698-2cf0-43f2-91df-cea8fc7f5e60
▶	2024-09-23T19:38:53.195Z	REPORT RequestId: 9813b698-2cf0-43f2-91df-cea8fc7f5e60 Duration: 583.57 ms Billed Duration: 584 m...

Back to top

16.   References

https://www.linkedin.com/pulse/salesforces-data-cloud-segmentation-andres-perez-eltoroit--kj6vc/

https://medium.com/salesforce-architects/4-considerations-for-salesforce-cdp-data-ingestion-c00af75167bc

https://data-mozart.com/parquet-file-format-everything-you-need-to-know/

https://www.salesforceblogger.com/2023/11/15/data-cloud-segmentation-best-practices/

https://www.salesforceben.com/key-salesforce-data-cloud-terms-to-know/

https://developer.salesforce.com/blogs/2023/08/bring-your-own-ai-models-to-salesforce-with-einstein-studio

https://help.salesforce.com/s/articleView?id=sf.c360_a_partyidentifier.htm&type=5